BEFORE
YOU
JUDGE
ME

BEFORE YOU JUDGE ME

THE TRIUMPH
AND TRAGEDY OF
MICHAEL JACKSON'S
LAST DAYS

TAVIS SMILEY
AND DAVID RITZ

LITTLE, BROWN AND COMPANY

New York   Boston   London

Little, Brown and Company
Hachette Book Group
1290 Avenue of the Americas, New York, NY 10104
littlebrown.com

First Edition: June 2016

Little, Brown and Company is a division of Hachette Book Group, Inc. The Little, Brown name and logo are trademarks of Hachette Book Group, Inc.

The publisher is not responsible for websites (or their content) that are not owned by the publisher.

The Hachette Speakers Bureau provides a wide range of authors for speaking events. To find out more, go to hachettespeakersbureau.com or call (866) 376-6591.

ISBN 978-0-316-25909-5

LCCN 2016930853

10 9 8 7 6 5 4 3 2

RRD-C

Printed in the United States of America

Contents

CONTENTS

Before you judge me
Try hard to love me

—"Childhood"
by Michael Jackson

BEFORE YOU JUDGE ME

Prologue

Wednesday, June 24, 2009

No one can quite believe it.

The dancers, the singers, the musicians, the crew—everyone is stunned, even shocked, by the power of Michael's performance. His presence has electrified the Staples Center. It makes no difference that the cavernous arena is empty. Makes no difference that this is only a rehearsal. What matters is that after months of dire uncertainty about the upcoming shows in London—months when the star has appeared too weak, distracted, or drugged to commit to this enormous undertaking—Michael has turned it around. Just when many were convinced that the concerts, starting July 13, would have to be scrubbed, Michael has proved the skeptics wrong.

His voice is strong. His dance moves are impeccable. His critiques of the arrangements and choreography are right on the mark. But what moves his support team most is Michael's heart. Everyone present can feel Michael's loving and generous heart. His heart is beating wildly, and so are theirs. In his heart, he has rededicated himself to the great task at hand.

Onstage, Michael has taken command of what only a few days earlier appeared to be a hopelessly unwieldy production. Only he knows how to repair and refit the broken pieces. Only he has the charismatic energy to bring it all together. Only he has the singular focus to salvage this enterprise and pull off the comeback he has promised his worldwide audience.

As he works his magic for hours on end, all eyes are on Michael. The renewal of his ambition — to make these shows the most spectacular in his four-decade history of performing — has excited the ambition of everyone around him. To be close to Michael is to be close to immortality.

When he leaves the Staples Center that Wednesday evening, exhausted but exhilarated, he feels more alive than ever.

Yet only sixteen weeks earlier, at a chaotic London press conference, he was experiencing far different feelings.

1

This Is It

On March 5, 2009, in London, England, Michael realizes he must do what he has long sought to avoid. He must announce his decision to return to the stage. At this point he has no choice. Commitments have been made, contracts signed. The deal is sealed. Yet part of him remains uncertain and reluctant. A fifty-year-old single father of three who has devoted himself to his children, he has for the past several years led a highly protected and insular family life. He has not toured since 1997 and not performed since 2006, and then only for a few fleeting moments. Following his dramatic acquittal after a sixteen-week-long trial in the summer of 2005, he and his children have wandered the world in search of a peace that has maddeningly eluded him. Meanwhile, with his finances in catastrophic disarray, he has finally settled upon a solution: a series of ten concerts at the O_2 Arena.

And still he isn't sure.

As hundreds of reporters and thousands of fans await

his arrival at the press conference inside the O$_2$, Michael paces back and forth in a van outside the arena. He is not ready to face the music or the worldwide media.

He cannot help but remember his last public appearance in London. It was in 2006, during the eighteenth annual World Music Awards. Beyoncé introduced him at Earls Court, where he was presented with a Guinness World Record: twenty-four years after its initial release, *Thriller* was declared the biggest-selling record ever. But what should have been a happy occasion turned sad—at least for Michael's fans. Besides joining with a children's choir to sing a few choruses of "We Are the World," Michael did nothing beyond give a brief acceptance speech. His fans had hoped he would perform "Thriller." Instead, it was Chris Brown who sang the song. The next day the press eviscerated Michael, who claimed that he had never been scheduled to sing. The negative publicity stung, and now, waiting in the van, Michael wonders whether London is ready to forgive and forget.

This announcement is a turning point. He knows that there's no going back. He's gone back before. Michael has a history of breaking commitments and canceling shows, followed by floods of legal entanglements. He can't afford to do that again.

"This is it" is the mantra that sounds inside his head.

This Is It is the actual name he's given the tour. He wants there to be no mistake.

This will be his last public performance.

Ever.

His closest confidants, like his sister Janet, understand who he is and who he will always be: an artist obsessed with art. He is a man who wants nothing more than the freedom to devote himself to making music and other creative endeavors. Live shows are simply too draining. They are repetitive. They reflect his past, not his present, and not his future.

The O_2 shows, though, will be different. He will not have to travel. This concert series will take place in one venue and one venue alone. That means he and his children can avoid the exhausting grind of a grueling tour.

The fact that his kids — Prince, twelve; Paris, ten; and Blanket, seven — have not seen the kind of jaw-dropping show he envisions for the O_2 fuels his drive. In these, his last performances, his children will at last experience a full-blown Michael Jackson spectacular. They will have that memory to cherish forever.

Michael definitely wants to perform for his children. But after the ten shows, he also wants to ensconce them in a sixteen-acre estate on Spanish Gate Drive in Las Vegas. This is the property he views as a replacement for Neverland, now associated with unbearable pain and ceaseless persecution. He is obsessed with owning this Vegas mansion, the ultimate sanctuary. But buying it from Prince Jefri Bolkiah, a member of the royal family of Brunei, will require the windfall income from This Is It — and then some.

So yes, Michael is motivated. He has every reason in the world to go out there and announce these ten shows. In his deepest heart, he still feels the great passion of his fans. For over forty years, he has experienced an extraordinary rapport with his admirers. Few entertainers have elicited such fierce loyalty. He loves them as much as they love him. He wishes to please, thrill, and satisfy them; he wishes to thank them for their unwavering support. No matter how bleak his circumstances, his fans have stood by his side, sung his praises, bought his records, come to his shows, slept in the cold streets outside his hotel rooms. In those instances, he has invariably sent them food and drink. After all-day, all-night plane rides, he has been known to stop and sign autographs for the fans who have come to greet him in Mumbai, Munich, or Amsterdam.

Why are his handlers, afraid that he has been drinking, so anxious about his state of mind? Why is he hesitating? Why is he so consumed with doubt? Why has he kept the crowd of reporters and fans waiting a half hour, now an hour, now nearly ninety minutes?

His reluctance is understandable. The shows' preparation will involve backbreaking work: arduous auditions, complex choreography, pyrotechnical special effects, meticulous musical preparations, and rigorous rehearsals. He sighs when he considers the road ahead. If only there was a way to avoid the ordeal. When AEG, the international entertainment promoter, initially proposed the idea of the O_2 concerts to Michael back in the spring of 2007, he expressed indifference. Negotiations were never initiated. But that was then, and this is now. Now, to satisfy his creditors and placate his fans, Michael has no choice.

He finds some comfort in the grand notion of destiny.

He sees the design of his immediate future formed by the same destiny that took shape decades earlier, when it became clear that, as a five-year-old, he would front the family band. Then — as now — destiny said, "Express your creative genius. Go out and perform. Wow the crowds. Make the people happy. Pay the bills. Work hard."

It is his destiny to return to the stage.

If he needs reassurance, it comes from a promotional film that he watches on a monitor in the van as it's simultaneously projected on giant screens in the O₂ Arena. It's a series of video clips designed to send Michael's fans, impatiently awaiting his delayed arrival, into hysteria.

The title card reads, "The time has come. The King of Pop returns."

Here is Michael — the militaristic Michael from the HIStory tour — carved in a heroic statue so gargantuan that helicopters fly beneath his spread-eagle legs.

Here is Michael negotiating his miraculous moonwalk during the musical break in "Billie Jean."

Here is red-leathered Michael forging a furiously syncopated peace among the warring "Beat It" gangs.

Here is Michael, as if shot through a cannon, leaping onstage during his *Dangerous* days.

Here is Michael prancing and prodding the ghouls and goblins in his sinuous "Thriller" dance.

Here is "Bad" Michael; "Dirty Diana" Michael; self-reflecting "Man in the Mirror" Michael; gravity-defying, mean-leaning "Smooth Criminal" Michael.

And all the while, in stadiums holding hundreds of

thousands of ecstatic spectators — from Budapest to Brunei, from Brisbane to Tunis, from Seoul to Johannesburg — fans scream and tremble, fans convulse, fans faint, fans are placed on stretchers and carried off because the mere sight of Michael Jackson — the sound of his soaring voice, the movement of his undulating body — is more than their consciousness can contain.

As Michael watches all this, his confidence is reinforced. He is reminded of his power as a performer. No matter how complex and painful the preparation, no matter how the shows mingle the present with the past, it's all worth it when he gets onstage and does what no one else can do.

He transcends. He transforms himself. He transforms the crowd. He loses himself, loses his doubts and apprehensions and becomes one with motion and melody. He moves through stages of ecstasy, and though extreme exhaustion follows every show, each one reestablishes the mystical harmony of his artistry. The extreme tensions of his personal life are worked out onstage: the pent-up rage, the mounting frustrations. If he embraces fury, grace can replace it. Lessons learned from the masters — from Fred Astaire and Charlie Chaplin and James Brown — are manifest in the form of a ferocious elegance, the hallmark of Michael Jackson's utterly unique style.

The promotional film has aroused him.

Now he is fortified. Now he is animated.

Now he is leaving the van and walking into the O$_2$ Arena.

Now he is facing the reporters and the hysterical fans.

Now he is smiling. Now he speaks.

"These will be my final performances. When I say this is it, it really means *this is it*."

In response to screams of "We love you, Michael!" he puts his hand over his heart and says, "I'll be performing the songs my fans want to hear... This is really it. This is the final curtain call. I love you, I really do. You have to know that. I love you so much from the bottom of my heart. This is it—and I'll see you in July."

He is up. He is happy. He is no longer equivocal.

It's all happening. He is back.

And minutes after his appearance, millions around the world prepare to assault the website that's selling tickets.

In one brief press conference, he has not only brought joy to fans, but he has given it to his children, his promoters, his managers, and himself.

He has embraced his destiny, a destiny that has always directed Michael Jackson toward spectacular success on the stage—the only place, he has claimed over and over again, where he feels entirely himself.

For the first time in years, he sees his future, once dark and foreboding, now bathed in the bright light of hope.

2

Who Will Buy This Wonderful Feeling?

To those who have dealt with him casually and those who have known him intimately, Michael Jackson is deeply loved. He is essentially a warmhearted, sweet, and gentle soul. Because he is extraordinarily sensitive, he is extraordinarily vulnerable. He is easily wounded. His instincts are to please. He dislikes confrontations and avoids them assiduously. He is smart, intuitive, and inexhaustibly curious. He loves the alchemy of art—the magic that informs theatricality of all kinds. He identifies with the powerless, especially children, and especially children who are thrust into the heady and exploitative world of entertainment.

It is only natural that on March 6, the Friday evening after his Thursday press conference, he has brought his children to London's Drury Lane theater to see the enormously entertaining *Oliver!*, whose subject matter is the cruel exploitation of children.

Because the drama unfolds in lighthearted musical form, what might otherwise be a repellent story is made palatable. The bleak is made merry. The ability to mutate nightmarish scenarios into dramas of delight is one of the great themes in the work of Michael Jackson. Seated in the theater, seeing joy in the faces of his children as the story plays out, he remembers the first time he saw the film adaptation of the play. It was at the end of the sixties. The movie *Oliver!* was named the best picture of 1968 at the Academy Awards held in 1969, the same year the Jackson 5 recorded its first number one hit, "I Want You Back," and released its first album. Michael viewed the movie at a moment when he couldn't help but relate to Mark Lester, who played Oliver Twist. Mark was nearly Michael's exact age. (Mark was born on July 11, 1958, Michael on August 29 the same year.) Like Michael, Mark won over audiences with a plaintive voice, an irresistible sweetness, and an engaging pluck.

Now, in the late winter of 2009, as Michael listens to Oliver sing "Where Is Love?," a lament for a lost mother, he is moved to tears. He thinks of his own mother, the one constant source of love in his childhood, and cannot imagine life without a steadying maternal presence. He considers the conditions for children in nineteenth-century London, homeless orphans forced into hard labor under subhuman conditions. He envisions the work of Lewis Hine, one of his favorite photographers, who in the early twentieth century documented the plight of children working in Pennsylvania coal mines, New York City sweatshops, Georgia textile mills, Virginia glass factories, and

Texas cotton fields. In Hine's stark photos, the eyes of the children are vacant. There is not a hint of hope. The light of love has been spent.

Michael relates to these children. He feels for them on the deepest level. He understands, remembering what it's like to be a child forced to labor under the uncaring hand of a brutal boss. But, while he knows that his talents were exploited, he also realizes that his particular exploitation was a complicated phenomenon — complicated because the work he was mandated to do, make music, brought him pleasure, recognition, and even adulation. Michael is left with the unsettling feeling that the exploitation might have been good for him.

It was music that took off the edge, just as another song sung by Oliver, "Who Will Buy?," takes the edge off the boy's dismal past through the expression of lilting melody. Melody washes away the pain and transforms what would be an intolerably painful story — the story of young Oliver Twist, or the story of young Michael Jackson — into a fable filled with optimism and good cheer.

It was a similarly sentimental musical number — "Climb Ev'ry Mountain" from *The Sound of Music* — that he remembers singing at his first public performance; it was at an elementary school assembly when he was six. No one explained the meaning of that song to him. No one had to. Aspirational energy was built into his character. He had to climb. He had to succeed. He still does.

Like so much of the art that Michael Jackson loves, *Oliver!* renews his spirit by affirming song and dance as the essential elements for overcoming trauma, no matter how severe. At every critical moment of his life, Michael has employed his musical genius to beat back the demons. It is the demons who drive the art — the manipulative villains like Fagin, who exploit children for personal profit, or, closer to home, his father, Joseph Jackson, whose beatings and attempts to terrorize Michael only added to his son's fierce ambition.

Like *The Sound of Music,* like all the minidramas created by Michael — from "Thriller" to *Captain EO* to *Ghosts* — *Oliver!* has a happy ending. Villains are vanquished. Evil falls beneath the power of the choreographed good guys. Like the "smooth criminal" he loves to portray, Michael always saves the day. He saves the children.

After the show, Michael takes his own three children from the theater back to the safety of the elegant Lanesborough hotel, where he receives word of the sudden death of his guitarist and friend, David Williams. The news shocks Michael and, as quick as that, throws him into a state of deep grief and reflection.

David, only fifty-eight, was felled by cardiac arrest. Michael remembers the first time he heard him play. It was on an R & B song, "Don't Hold Back," by the group Chanson. David's relentless rhythm guitar line riveted Michael's attention. It was 1978, and, in conjunction with Quincy Jones, twenty-year-old Michael was auditioning musicians for what would be the first Jackson-Jones collaboration, *Off the Wall.* When David showed up at Cherokee Studios in Los Angeles, he was presented with a rough version of "Rock with You" and asked to provide a guitar part. His playing stunned Michael. David's rhythm riffs were complex, brilliantly percussive, and slyly seductive. David was precisely what Michael was looking for: a guitarist whose grooves both anchored and propelled the melody. That paradox — locating a rhythm locked in time and yet one that thrusts time forward, a rhythm that seemingly explodes time — is at the heart of Michael's music.

At the end of the seventies, pop music was dominated by disco, a phenomenon that Michael embraced when he wrote and produced songs like "Blame It on the Boogie" and "Shake Your Body (Down to the Ground)" for the Jacksons. When he encountered Quincy in 1977 while making his film debut as the dancing scarecrow in *The Wiz*, Michael decided that Jones, with his eclectic background in jazz, pop, and soul, was a master musician under whom he should work. Like Michael, Quincy was committed to a marriage of art and commerce. He wanted to make great music, but music that sold. Neither harbored any doubts about staying true to the demands of dance music. Dance music, after all, had been Michael's calling card since the first three number one Jackson 5 records — "I Want You Back," "ABC," and "The Love You Save" — were designed for the dance floor. The boy band was shaped both sonically and sartorially under the heavy influence of Sly and the Family Stone, the best and most boldly revolutionary dance band to emerge in the late sixties. Sly was seen as the greatest groovemeister since James Brown.

Brown was Michael's first and mightiest musical master.

In 1963, young Michael had already committed to memory Brown's *Live at the Apollo*. From watching James Brown on television, Michael had also learned the slickest of his dance moves.

"The little squirt did James Brown better than JB himself," recalled Bobby Taylor, leader of the Vancouvers, a Motown soul band that included Tommy Chong, later of Cheech and Chong, on guitar. Taylor, a superb singer himself, discovered the Jackson 5 in 1968, when they played the Regal Theater in Chicago.

Michael "broke out in a 'Cold Sweat,'" said Bobby. "He sang 'I Got the Feelin'" with feelings you can't fake. He tore up the stage like JB's long lost love child—the spins, the mic action, the fall-on-your-knees-and-beg-for-it moves. His voice grabbed me by the throat and said, 'Take me to your heart. Take me to your leader.' So right after the show, I did just that. I jumped up and told his dad, 'Joe, we're off to Detroit.'"

A few months later, the Jackson 5 was produced by Taylor, who had brought them to Detroit, where Berry Gordy signed them.

"I saw the J5 as a straight-up soul group," said Taylor. "That's what I knew and loved—and that's what they knew and loved. Mike went to bed with James Brown and Jackie Wilson records under his pillow. The rest of the brothers idolized Smokey and Marvin. Like their old man, the kids were products of the great tradition. It was in my blood—and theirs—to cherish that tradition while taking it to the next level. It was my job to feed Mike's soul."

But Taylor's initial Jackson 5 productions, while vocal

gems, were seen by Gordy as soul-centric and thus commercially limited.

"When we promoted our acts in the sixties, we explicitly avoided the word 'soul,'" said Michael Roshkind, one of Gordy's closest lieutenants. "We wanted pop. Pop was the crossover dream, the golden goose. You'll notice how decades later, when Michael hit his stride around the world, he didn't name himself King of Soul. He crowned himself King of Pop. He got that pop fixation from Berry."

"One night Bobby had Michael in the studio singing Clyde McPhatter's 'Money Honey' when Berry walked in," remembered Motown producer Hal Davis. "Berry told Bobby he was making a mistake by restricting them to R & B. Berry wanted pop songs. In his spitfire manner, Bobby gave Berry the finger. Then Berry gave Bobby the boot."

By moving the boys from Detroit to Los Angeles, where he had relocated, Gordy took over their career. He joined the Corporation, a songwriters' collective led by Deke Richards, who composed the initial string of Jackson 5 hits that captured the irresistible funk of Sly's polypercussive playfulness and established the group as a pop act.

In studying James Brown and Sly and the Family Stone, young Michael Jackson realized the critical importance of rhythm guitar. That's why, at the end of the seventies, a decade after he had been signed to Motown and poised to make his first solo record for CBS/Epic, Michael was delighted to discover in David Williams a guitarist whose seamless grooves inspired not only his dance moves but his singing as well.

David became a steady presence in Michael's musical life. In *Off the Wall*, he embellished "Don't Stop 'Til You Get Enough," "Rock with You," "Working Day and Night," and the title tune. Three years later, in 1982, he contributed mightily to the feel of "Wanna Be Startin' Somethin'," "Baby Be Mine," and "Thriller." Most famously, it was David's guitar solo that electrified "Billie Jean." He also played all over *Bad*, *Dangerous*, and *HIStory*. He was Michael's go-to rhythm guitarist on each of his world tours, from Victory in 1984 to HIStory in 1996.

In his London hotel in early March of 2009, Michael is devastated by the news of David Williams's death. A remarkably nuanced musician himself, Michael is aware of the significance of subtlety in the structure of song and the design of dance. Michael will miss David's singular touch, especially during these upcoming This Is It shows.

Death — unwelcomed and unexpected death — robs Michael of his peace of mind. He goes to the bedrooms of his children and sees that they are sleeping peacefully. But he cannot sleep, not while his mind is assaulted by thoughts of loss.

3

Stranger in Moscow

On March 8, during the long plane ride from London to Los Angeles, while his children read books and play video games, Michael sits back and listens with headphones to a song he wrote sixteen years earlier. It's a brooding meditation on loneliness in which he sees himself walking the streets of Moscow, wandering in the rain, feeling somewhat insane, and contemplating his fall from grace. Fame, he feels, has abandoned him. He fears what he calls an "Armageddon of the brain."

Although "Stranger in Moscow" is a sad song — you might even call it a dirge — its slow, steady rhythms comfort Michael as the private jet wings its way over the vast and brooding Atlantic Ocean. Writing the song while in Russia in 1993, during the Dangerous tour, he felt his world collapsing around him. Although not a formal blues, the song embraces the blues aesthetic so close to Michael's musical heart.

"Michael will never lose the quality that separates the

merely sentimental from the truly heartfelt," Marvin Gaye once said. "It's rooted in the blues, and no matter what genre Michael is singing, the boy's got the blues."

"I taught Michael that the best way to rid yourself of those down and dirty blues is to get hold of a down and dirty song and sing the hell out of it," said Bobby Taylor. "So I gave him Ray Charles's 'A Fool for You,' one of Ray's down-est and dirtiest. Mind you, Michael recorded it when he was eleven years old. Yet he nailed it. That's because when he was a kid he was really a grown man with grown-up feelings, and when he grew up and became a man he was really a kid with kid-like feelings."

Now, with the long flight in front of him, Michael is feeling unusually calm, as though listening to his own lament to loneliness — a song written in the depths of despair — clarifies his current, improved condition. He was a stranger in Moscow during a time — September of 1993 — when the child molestation charges brought against him were still pending. He felt isolated and vulnerable. A month later, in a nursing home in Phoenix, his grand-father Samuel Jackson died. Michael was obsessed with loss and filled with fears. He was also heavily sedated.

On November 12, 1993, he decided he could take no more and reached out for help. He canceled the rest of the Dangerous tour. Accompanied by Elizabeth Taylor and Larry Fortensky, whom the actress had met at the Betty Ford Center and married at Neverland two years earlier, Michael flew from Mexico City to London, where, after conferring with Elton John, the artist took his recommendation and checked into the Charter Nightingale Clinic.

The next day Pepsi ended its decadelong relationship with Michael.

On November 16, 1993, the *New York Times* reported on a press conference at which Michael's lawyer announced that Michael was in intensive treatment for his addiction to "very, very heavy-duty" prescription painkillers. The attorney further explained that Michael began taking the sedatives after being burned during the making of a Pepsi commercial in 1984.

Back at home five weeks later, Michael released Live from Neverland Valley, a televised explanation. With focused determination, he spoke about his recent treatment for drug dependency. He repeated the backstory: "This medicine was initially prescribed to soothe the excruciating pain that I was suffering after recent reconstructive surgery on my scalp." He called the charges against him "disgusting" and "totally false" and complained about the "dehumanizing and humiliating examination" made by the Santa Barbara County Sheriff's Office and the Los Angeles Police Department. He concluded by recounting his long history of trying "to help thousands upon thousands of children to live happy lives" and quoted Jesus: "'Suffer little children to come unto me, and forbid them not, for such is the kingdom of heaven.' In no way do I think that I am God, but I do try to be God-like in my heart."

Five weeks after this statement, the case against him was settled out of court.

Four months later, he married Lisa Marie Presley.

Now, in March of 2009, Michael is flying home from London, just as he flew home from London after his rehab stay in 1993. As the chorus of "Stranger in Moscow" drowns out the drone of the jet engines, he reflects upon the difference between the present and the past. In 1994, his back was to the wall. Pundits said he was through. They said he'd never come back. But he did. He worked through the depression depicted so poignantly in "Stranger in Moscow." In that song, he wrote of the danger he faced and the loneliness he felt. "We're talkin' danger, baby," he cried. "I'm livin' lonely, baby!"

Yet he emerged from the emotional morass and found the strength to start a new project, *HIStory*, on which "Stranger in Moscow" is the signature song. *HIStory* became his most autobiographical and introspective work to date. His mind-set was clear: He would not crack up. He would not break down. He would not only face the music — the ongoing assumptions about his aberrant behavior — but make startling new music into which he would infuse all his bravado, anger, fears, and faith. He would turn confusion into art.

"Scream" was the leadoff single from the album, a duet with sister Janet and the first song Michael released in the wake of the allegations against him. Written with Janet and Janet's producers, Jimmy Jam and Terry Lewis, the song was Michael's first musical response to the events of the previous two years. Beyond hitting number one and disproving predictions of Michael's demise in the market-place, "Scream" was a Grammy Award–winning video directed by Mark Romanek. It was a wildly creative fantasy about the way in which Michael deals with the pressures inside his head.

At the time of the video's release — the midnineties — Janet is at the height of her popularity. As she poses, sings, and dances by her brother's side, she does more than support him; she lends him her own unchecked audacity. Trapped inside a futuristic vessel hurtling through space, they scream to be released from the pressures of a planet overrun by injustice and corrupted by a system fueled by lies. Dressed like Nikita, the fearless action heroine–assassin, Janet tackles the role of superaggressive sister protecting her brother under assault. Facing the camera, facing a world that would scorn and judge Michael, she flips the bird. She boldly assumes the macho stance of a scrapper as she positions herself in front of a urinal. There's a strong sense of gender-bending, a notion that Michael and Janet, two extraordinary creatures, are too singular to be understood by ordinary human beings. Inside the space pod, in which they are both prisoners and artistic pioneers, they are able to access praying Buddhas, ancient sculpture, surreal paintings by Magritte, and pop art by Andy Warhol. All the while, an enraged Michael is smashing guitars and shattering vases. Even as "Scream" bemoans the pressures of being a Jackson, pressure is released and metamorphosed in a space odyssey drama set to furious syncopation.

Metamorphosis is not only at the heart of Michael's art; it is his salvation. It was true in the summer of 1995 and remains even truer here in the late winter of 2009. Ruminating on the towering obstacles he has already met and conquered, he knows he can do it again. He can do it because he can change, mutate, mold trauma into healing melody and heartache into joyful dance. Artistically, he has been changing—and advancing—since he was six. His initial work with the Jackson 5 led to even more astounding solo work that included masterpieces of the early seventies like "Ben" and "I Wanna Be Where You Are." When the brothers left Motown for CBS's Epic label, Michael assiduously cultivated his talents as a writer and producer. The Jacksons' *Destiny*, released in 1978, only a year before *Off the Wall*, is a testament to his commitment to honing his studio skills. From *Off the Wall* to *Thriller* (1982) to *Bad* (1987) to *Dangerous* (1991) to *HIStory* (1995) to *Blood on the Dance Floor* (1997) to *Invincible* (2001) to the songs he has recently written, the artistic curve is up, up, up. His work has grown in complexity, brilliance, and courage.

"Everyone knew Michael was the greatest child vocalist who's ever lived," said Smokey Robinson, who first heard him when Bobby Taylor brought the brothers to Detroit in 1968. "We knew he loved to learn from everyone around him. We saw him watching us from the wings. It was clear that he was absorbing everything from the performers he admired most. But what we didn't know was that it wasn't enough for him to outdo his colleagues. That was fine. That was the Motown credo that said competition breeds champions. But what blew me away was his drive not to best us but to always best himself. That's why, as a singer and songwriter and producer and dancer, he kept growing, kept getting better, kept looking to reach a mountaintop that kept getting higher and higher."

"The difference between me and Michael Jackson," Rick James once explained, "is that my music can be contaminated and Michael's can't. I'm not saying that I don't think I'm great. I know I'm great. But I also know that I'm no purist. I don't mind putting in a lick or a lyric not because I love it, but because I know it'll sell. Michael's incapable of doing that. He has to express his heart and mind exactly the way he's feeling it. He's pure. He's the best and only example I know of a soul singer who's an absolutely pure artist. I think that's why he became bigger than any of us. When the world hears purity, they respond to it. They go crazy. A pure spirit is the most powerful spirit. But what happens to a pure spirit when that spirit has to move through an impure world? Sometimes I think that our world, filled with nasty poisons, can't stand purity and ain't happy till the purity and all the pure artists are wiped off the face of the earth."

The long plane ride is practically over. Michael is glad to have this quick trip to London behind him. Glad to have finally made the decision. Glad to have announced the concerts at the O$_2$. Glad to see the reception so overwhelmingly warm and positive. Glad that he brought his children so that they can share in the mounting excitement surrounding this series of shows. Glad that, after years in the wilderness, he finally feels in control of his life.

The plane lands. Michael and the children are driven to their temporary home at 100 North Carolwood Drive in the exclusive Holmby Hills section of Los Angeles. This is the seven-bedroom, thirteen-bathroom mansion for which AEG, promoter of the O$_2$ shows, is paying $100,000 a month to house Michael and the kids.

Michael hopes that, after the long flight, he will be able to sleep. But after he has read the kids stories, kissed and cuddled them in bed, he's unable to curtail the thoughts racing in his head. In his master bedroom, he looks over the messages that have piled up in his absence and feels optimism slipping away. Virtually all the messages can be ignored, but the most insistent ones are troubling. They come from a man who demands that Michael see him immediately. These are the messages from his father, Joseph.

His father and the pressures brought to bear upon Michael from his family of origin are among the real reasons he vowed not to return to Southern California after the long and arduous trial that ended with his acquittal nearly four years earlier in Santa Barbara. Although his family supported him throughout the ordeal, he knew that allowing them back into his life, whether in a personal or professional capacity, always meant heartache. At the same time, excluding them never failed to fill him with painful guilt.

Guilt is the card that his family has played ever since the early eighties, when *Thriller* turned Michael into the biggest star on the planet. It was after the megasuccess of *Thriller* that their pressure got to him. He caved in and reluctantly agreed to cut one more album with his siblings, *Victory*, followed by the chaotic Jacksons tour in 1984. Michael was miserable throughout the ordeal — not because he didn't love his brothers, but because the great love he felt for them no longer translated into a viable creative relationship.

Like his sister Janet, he craves control of his artistic product and freedom from family meddling. But unlike Janet — who, after expelling Joseph from her business life, never let him back in — Michael equivocates. He wants to make his mother happy, which means placating his brothers and ultimately his father as well.

There are dark memories from his childhood but sweet ones as well. In his heart he carries the conviction that all families should be close and loving, and yet history has shown him that his own family, torn apart by dissension and jealousy, can never be trusted to bring him solace. In fact, time and again, his family has brought him grief.

Grief keeps him up tonight — grief about the times he's tried to reconcile with his brothers and father, the times he's sought to forge a peace, the times he's tried, mostly in vain, to establish healthy boundaries. But over and over again, boundaries have been violated, and in the end, he has felt that, aside from Janet, each of his family members wants to claim a piece of him.

The thought of betrayal keeps him up tonight. He's haunted by memories of how, in 1991, in reaction to the worldwide success of *Bad*, brother Jermaine released a reply record—"Word to the Badd!!"—accusing Michael of self-centeredness and unscrupulous careerism. Two years later, when accusations of pedophilia first emerged, sister La Toya threw him under the bus by publicly giving credence to the rumors.

He can't sleep because the forces he escaped by leaving the country after his 2005 acquittal are still in place in 2009. Confusing matters more, many of his old nemeses have become allies. Brother Jermaine, for instance, is the one who introduced him to Tohme Tohme, his present manager, who brought in AEG, the organization investing a fortune in salvaging Michael's finances.

He can't sleep tonight because he's unable to forget the series of events—improbable and unpredictable—that has led him to be living in this house in Holmby Hills.

For the past four years he has been running, ducking, and hiding.

Close to a physical and emotional breakdown at the end of the trial in the summer of 2005, he rejected the idea of returning to Neverland. Instead, he took his kids and flew to the other side of the world, to Bahrain, in the Persian Gulf, where he lived off the largesse of Sheikh Abdullah, whom he had also met through Jermaine, a Muslim since converting in 1989. For a while it appeared as if the sheikh was just the wealthy patron Michael had long sought. Together they forged a company with ambitious plans to make music and movies. But the harmony between the soul singer and the Arab royal lasted less than a year.

After Michael took the kids to Tokyo in the summer of 2006 for the MTV awards show, he never returned to Bahrain. His relationship with the sheikh, who eventually sued Michael, was shattered. The next chapter in his sojourn unfolded in the remote Irish countryside, where, from August through the end of the year, he worked with artists, among them Will.i.am, on new music. It was there that magician Liam Sheehan entertained Michael and his kids for days on end. Magic held the same fascination for Michael as music. He saw them as similar phenomena.

Toward the end of 2006, Michael and the children flew from Dublin to Las Vegas, where he rented a house on Monte Cristo Way. The hope was that in Vegas, with its enormous venues and insatiable appetite for splashy entertainment, he would find a promoter to keep his sinking financial ship afloat. No matter how great his net worth — estimates ran as high as $236 million — Michael's debts were far higher. He was indeed courted by many of the most powerful men in the city, but he wasn't ready to go back onstage. He turned down all offers.

On December 30, 2006, Michael flew to Augusta, Georgia, for the funeral of James Brown, to pay homage to the master. Michael spoke of James as his single greatest influence and spent an inordinate amount of time in a private room with James's corpse. Then it was back to Vegas, where his father, Joseph, and brother Randy, who briefly managed Michael around the time of the 2005 trial, desperately tried to gain entrance to the Monte Cristo compound. They wanted to reestablish a business relationship with Michael, but Michael wouldn't let them in.

Michael lay low in Vegas during the first few months of 2007. By June he was in the Washington, DC, area, living in hotels and looking for a home. With his finances more precarious than ever, he maxed out his credit cards. Hotels refused his business. In August, with his children in tow, he went to live in suburban New Jersey with the Cascios, his beloved surrogate family, with whom he'd been extraordinarily close for decades. A couple of months later, he and the kids relocated to Los Angeles, where he attended Jesse Jackson's sixty-sixth birthday party. Meanwhile, Sheikh Abdullah sued Michael for $7 million.

During the Thanksgiving and Christmas holidays of 2007, billionaire Ron Burkle, whom Michael met through Jesse Jackson, volunteered to look into Michael's financial morass. Michael was in imminent danger of losing his most valuable assets: Neverland and the Sony/ATV song catalog that included the Beatles' copyrights. Meanwhile, Burkle arranged for Michael and the children to stay at Green Acres, the billionaire's sprawling Los Angeles estate, free of charge.

By the end of 2007, Michael was able to refinance his loans and save his properties. He returned to Las Vegas, living at the Palms Casino Resort. He went to work at a recording studio, where he began developing new material.

In February of 2008, he was encouraged by the successful release of the twenty-fifth-anniversary edition of *Thriller*.

In March, he and the children moved to still another Vegas rental property, a house on Palomino Lane. That's when Michael met billionaire Tom Barrack, who looked at his debt — by then some $400 million — and decided to save the Neverland ranch and also connect Michael to another billionaire, Philip Anschutz, owner of AEG Live, the concert promoter. It didn't take the Barrack-Anschutz team long to envision the enormous earning potential in terms of Michael Jackson world concert tours, movies, amusement parks, and even casinos. They were willing to pour tens of millions into rebuilding the Michael Jackson brand.

Michael's introductions to Barrack and Anschutz were facilitated by Lebanese-born businessman Tohme Tohme.

By the summer of 2008, Raymone Bain, Michael's manager during his posttrial period in the Middle East and Ireland, had been dismissed, and Tohme Tohme installed as her replacement.

That fall, father Joseph reentered the picture, pressuring Michael to join a Jackson family reunion concert promoted by Patrick Allocco's AllGood Entertainment. Allocco was also meeting with still another former Michael Jackson manager, Frank Dileo.

In December of 2008, Michael moved from Vegas to the Carolwood estate in Los Angeles — the same estate where he now tries to sleep, after returning from London and the announcement of the This Is It shows, on this March night in 2009.

He's been through a lot in just a few years.

From Bahrain to Tokyo. From Tokyo to Ireland.

From Ireland to Vegas. From Vegas to DC.

From DC to New Jersey and the solace of the Cascios' home.

From Jersey to L.A. and then back to Vegas before returning to L.A.

And now all focus is on London.

He has four months to prepare.

Four months to deal with the forces at play: his manager, his family, his creditors, his promoters.

Four months to make good on a deal that will surely secure for him the dream house — Prince Jefri's mansion in Las Vegas — where he and his children can live happily ever after.

Four months to rehearse for a series of shows — he has to do only ten — that will repay his loving fans for their unwavering loyalty.

Four months to reassert his reputation as the world's greatest entertainer.

Four months to get in control of his life.

Four months to finally put behind him the confusion and pain of his recent past.

Four months to do what he has always been able to do: put his mind and heart into his art.

Four months to reestablish his sense of purpose.

Yes, Michael tells himself, *four months is enough. Four months is all I need.*

And yet he still can't sleep.

4

Demerol

Back in 1997, at the conclusion of his third and final international solo tour — this one in support of the *HIStory* project — Michael released *Blood on the Dance Floor*, an album that included five new songs and eight remixes of previous releases. Among the new material was "Morphine," the first and only Michael Jackson song to deal with his relationship to drugs.

He thinks of "Morphine" on March 12, 2009, when he is on his way to the office of Dr. Arnold Klein, the dermatologist he met back in the eighties through entertainment mogul David Geffen. Although Michael has requested that AEG employ Dr. Conrad Murray, who occasionally treated his children for minor ailments in Vegas, as his full-time, live-in physician, he turns to Klein when he feels the need to escape the pain in his body and mind.

There was a time when Klein's clients, among them Michael's dear friend Elizabeth Taylor, saw him as a savior. Klein and Michael were especially close. It was in Klein's office that Michael met Debbie Rowe, his second wife and the mother of his first two children. Klein gained a national reputation for his use of Botox to augment lips and remove wrinkles and crow's-feet from the face. Obsessed with appearing forever young, Michael turned to Klein—as well as to plastic surgeon Dr. Steven Hoefflin—to maintain a youthful appearance. Michael wanted, among other features, an upturned nose—much like the nose of Bobby Driscoll, the child actor hired by Disney to be the voice and likeness of Peter Pan—and a cleft in his chin and a blemish-free complexion. As a teenager, Michael, like Bobby Driscoll, was tortured by chronic outbreaks of acne. And as an adult, Michael was alarmed by an ongoing condition of vitiligo, a disease causing blotches of pigmentation loss. He feared that he would be permanently marred. After meeting Klein, the doctor who cleared up his skin, Michael felt relief and gratitude. But beyond the Botox and assorted collagens, Klein gave Michael something else: Demerol.

Demerol is a powerful painkilling opioid, an addictive narcotic. Ever since the near-tragic accident that scorched Michael's scalp in 1984, he has relied on medicine to cope with pain. This is the same reliance that caused him to cut short his Dangerous tour and enter a rehab facility in the early nineties. Among his close friends and family members, it is common knowledge that he has slowly slipped back into Demerol dependence. Interventions have proved unsuccessful.

"Morphine" is one of Michael's major musical constructions. It's both frighteningly raw and hauntingly ethereal. Its

36

story line is intentionally opaque. The drug is seen as a "hot kiss," a "hot buzz," a "kick in the back," a "heart attack." The sonic atmosphere is startling—a heady mixture of joy and shame, desire and remorse, dismay and relief. After he sings the first few verses with shocking intensity, Michael drifts off into a remarkable reverie. The beat suddenly stops. Rhythm is suspended. And suddenly he's ingesting the drug and describing a state of euphoria. He surrenders to the high and melodically replicates the floating feeling brought on by Demerol. "Demerol," he sings over and over again, looking down at himself in an out-of-body moment. "Oh, God, he's taking Demerol!" He floats out into space; he floats above all physical distress, entering a stratosphere of pure pleasure. But the respite is brief. The interlude ends and we're back into the endless warfare between willpower and indulgence, ecstasy and disease.

Today Michael's need to escape is great. After his return from London, his equivocation about the This Is It shows has grown. That's because yesterday, March 11, he was told that all ten shows sold out in record time. The overwhelming demand crashed the websites where tickets were offered. Given Michael's financial needs, Tohme Tohme and AEG argued that it would be foolish not to add another ten shows. They also let it be known that Prince held the record of selling out the O_2, with twenty-one straight shows. They were certain that this fact would stoke Michael's competitive fires and motivate him to do at least thirty shows, if only to best the artist with whom he has been compared since the early eighties.

Michael agrees to thirty concerts, but when they sell out as quickly as the first ten, he's given a new number: fifty. No one has ever come close to selling out the O_2 with fifty consecutive shows. At first Michael is furious. That's outrageous, far beyond anything he would ever consider. The task is too great; the work will be crushing. But his handlers spell out the tremendous financial rewards. They also appeal to his sense of grand destiny. If one man can sell out fifty shows at the O_2, they contend, that man is Michael Jackson.

They know how to push his buttons. After much heated discussion, Michael submits, but with one caveat: AEG must guarantee the presence of people from the Guinness World Records book to formally mark all the record-breaking accomplishments.

So somehow, within a span of days, Michael has committed to five times as many shows as originally planned. He knows full well that his crafty handlers are manipulating him. But he also knows that he's getting 90 percent of the profits from the concerts. In these new negotiations, he has also been able to get AEG to put down $15 million in a fund toward buying Prince Jefri's Vegas mansion.

The result of this last-minute inflation of obligations is confusion. On one hand, there is Michael the Conqueror, Michael who wants to break every sales record ever set, Michael who set his sights on world dominion. This is the same Michael who, in drumming up excitement for his HIStory tour, ordered the construction of a colossal statue of himself, in mock military garb, and had it set upon a barge that floated down the River Thames. This is the Michael who called himself the Thriller, called himself Bad, called himself Dangerous, and won't stop until he rewrites the pages of HIStory to include a chapter on his unmatched feats. This is Michael the Heroic, Michael who, in 2001, titled his most recent studio album *Invincible*. This is the strong, determined, forward-looking, forward-marching, unbeatable, intractable Michael.

But there's another Michael, a realistic Michael, a humble Michael, a Michael who realizes that he has limits, a Michael who, from long experience, knows that the task of performing shows in a relatively short span of time, even without the rigors of moving from city to city, can be crushing. This is a Michael who remembers the fatigue suffered after three mind-numbing, soul-draining world tours: Bad, Dangerous, and HIStory. This is a Michael who realizes that he's physically out of shape and emotionally out of sorts, a Michael who, out of the corner of his eye, sees his father making a move on him, a Michael who wishes he had kept his vow never to return to Southern California, the place where his fortunes fell so precipitously in 1993, with allegations of pedophilia and, a decade later, with an arrest and a prolonged trial. This is a Michael who wants to escape, slip back into hiding, and flee to an obscure corner of the world, where no one and nothing can ever bother him again.

One Michael is excited by the notion of his own grandiosity. That Michael can't get enough attention. Another Michael seeks solace in solitude. That Michael longs for anonymity. The conflict is hardly new. And adding to the puzzlement is that both Michaels—the one seeking the spotlight and the one running from it—have a heart to help a world full of hurt, have ambition to heal an ailing planet. Michael the Conqueror sees himself as strong enough to make a meaningful difference, just as Modest Michael, without pomp or ceremony, is moved to lend a hand to a homeless child or an impoverished orphan.

"Before *Off the Wall,* when Michael could still step out in public without being mobbed, we'd go to a vegetarian restaurant called the Golden Temple," said sister Janet. "He'd buy a large quantity of take-out meals, and we'd spend an entire afternoon riding around the city, stopping and giving this food to the homeless. We'd do this day after day. He'd say, 'I know this is just a drop in the bucket. There's still so much suffering in the world, but at least we're doing something.' When I watched him do all this, I realized that, for all his conflicts, he had an absolutely pure heart."

"Michael's good-heartedness worked for him and against him," said Bobby Taylor, the man who discovered him. "It worked for him because he was a truly wonderful human being with tremendous empathy for everyone. But it worked against him, I believe, because it made him want to please everyone—starting with his father. If you trace Michael's career, you see him always working his tail off to please some kind of authority figure standing over him. After his father, it was Berry Gordy. After Berry Gordy, it was Quincy Jones. While with Quincy, there was also Walter

Yetnikoff, the big boss at CBS Records. Eventually Michael did become more his own man — his own producer and his own boss — but that little kid inside him that was dying to please Daddy never completely died. And, of course, when it comes to Michael's mother, Miss Katherine, he'd do anything in the world to make her happy. She held more sway over her son than anyone.

"If you want to understand Michael, you got to remember one thing: he can be gotten to. By that I mean that he's easily influenced. And he's easily influenced because he's basically a nice guy who wants to make you happy. He's also easily influenced because he's a genuinely curious and open-minded individual. So if you can get close to Michael, and if you exert a powerful authoritative vibe, chances are you can get him to go along with your program. That's why he's had so many different managers at so many different times telling him what to do. And that's why all these people, looking for a piece of the pie, went crazy trying to get next to him. They knew that once they had his ear, there was a good chance they'd also get his money."

During the short ride from the Carolwood estate to the office of Dr. Arnold Klein in Beverly Hills, Michael is all too aware of the people looking to get next to him. Now that he is back in Los Angeles, the center of the entertainment world, he feels that world crowding in on him. People from his past—managers, agents, and lawyers he once dismissed—are now knocking at his door. The voices inside Michael's head are as loud and dissonant as ever.

You need to avoid these people, says one voice. *There's a good reason why you cut them off. They were too self-serving, too controlling. Don't get bit by the same dog twice.*

But another voice says, *You need to allow these people back in your life. They helped you prosper. They served at a time when, unlike now, you were at the top of the charts.*

And a third voice: *More than ever, you need strong guidance. You've made a mess out of your finances, and you lack the knowledge and wisdom to fix the problem.*

And a fourth voice: *No one can solve the dilemma except you. You know yourself. You've always known what to do. You've always come back. This time will be no different.*

This time is different, says still another voice. *This time you've bitten off more than you can chew. Committing to fifty shows is crazy. Your advisors are crazy.*

Fifty shows is sensational, argues a countervoice. *Your advisors are sensational. They're saving your life.*

You're ruining your life.

You're gaining your life back.

You've never been stronger.

You've never felt weaker.

The voices need to stop, and there's only one way to stop them.

"Demerol," the song says. "Oh, God, he's taking Demerol."

Thus on the twelfth of March, in the privacy of Dr. Klein's office, Michael is given Demerol to assuage the discomfort associated with minor dermatological procedures on his chin. Typically, a patient would receive fifty milligrams, but Michael, who over the years has developed a high tolerance for the narcotic, ingests two hundred milligrams.

The vicious and confusing voices are quieted.

The pain subsides.

5

Jehovah

Three days after the appointment with Klein, it is Sunday, March 15. Michael is at home with the kids, watching cartoons and reading books. There's nothing he enjoys more than the company of his children.

His manager, Tohme Tohme, feeds him positive reports from the press. From the *London Evening Standard*, there are ecstatically optimistic statements from Randy Phillips, the AEG exec in charge of Michael's This Is It shows. When it comes to Michael's health, Phillips is unreservedly upbeat.

"Michael was put through a whole battery of tests," he says. "Stress, treadmill, electrocardiogram, blood work, and he passed them all... He's in very good health. I'm fifty-four, he's fifty, and I would like to have his cholesterol levels... He look[s] great. He's filled out a little. He's training."

Lou Ferrigno, who starred in TV's *The Incredible Hulk*, is due to come over and start Michael on a fitness routine. Beyond that, Michael has hired a personal chef and is committed to a healthier eating program that excludes the greasy fried chicken he loves so much.

The campaign is in place: vigorous exercise, nutritious food, and the mounting of the greatest shows of his career. Michael has reason to be of good cheer. Today his mind is clear. He's wished away thoughts of the brewing warfare between rival handlers. He's ignored the onslaught of urgent messages from his father, demanding a meeting. It's Sunday, after all, and Sunday is the Sabbath, the day when even God Almighty rested.

Sunday inevitably brings back thoughts of the Jehovah's Witnesses and services at the Kingdom Hall where Michael's mother brought her children to worship. After studying scripture for three years, Katherine was baptized as a Witness at age thirty-three, in 1963, around the time that five-year-old Michael began singing with his brothers. In her autobiography, written at the height of Michael's fame in the late eighties, Katherine explained that her conversion started "with a knock on my door." She was receptive to the evangelist's strict understanding of biblical law. There was no ambiguity, no uncertainty. All questions were answered. The Witnesses proclaimed that these were the final days. After the imminent battle of Armageddon, only the true believers would be spared. Katherine was moved to become a true believer, and further moved to make certain that her children believed as well.

Michael didn't simply love his mother; he adored her. While his father employed brutal corporal punishment, his mother showered him with affection. And when his mother claimed that she had found the only true path to God, Michael followed her down that path with unswerving faith. His mother was incapable of falsehood. When she explained that Jehovah was to be sought and found through the teachings of the Witnesses, Michael, the most devoted of all her sons, accepted her explanation wholeheartedly.

Michael saw Joseph as a restless and furious man. He saw Katherine as a serene and gentle woman. Joseph's role was to prepare him to enter the ruthless world of show business. Katherine's role was to prepare him to enter the hallowed Kingdom of God.

That Joseph both realized and, at the same time, undermined that showbiz preparation is a difficult dichotomy for Michael to accept. Michael did, of course, succeed beyond anyone's wildest expectations. But the success was destabilized when, time and again, Michael was overwhelmed by the insane demands of show business and barely able to operate. Joseph was never capable of giving his son the necessary inner resources to effectively deal with stellar achievement.

Although Michael will never publicly say so, Katherine's spiritual preparation has also proved problematic. Just as Joseph's program of nonstop work to achieve stardom was based on an uncompromising austerity, so was Katherine's religion. Aside from the memorial of the Last Supper, the Witnesses eschew all holidays, including Christmas and birthdays. What they consider secular celebrations are strictly forbidden. Joseph enforced an unbending discipline in the realm of entertainment: practice, practice, practice.

In the realm of spirituality, Katherine demanded another form of strict discipline: submit, submit, submit.

As a child, whenever Michael was home, he clung to his mother. As an adult, he continued to live at home — and was the primary provider for his nuclear family — until 1988, when, at nearly thirty, he finally moved out of the Encino estate on Hayvenhurst Avenue and into Neverland. It's easy to understand why Michael found it difficult to leave his mother's side. She made him feel whole; she made him feel safe. Adopting the authoritarian interpretations of scripture taught by the Witnesses, she offered Michael answers that seemed at once simple and profound. As late as the 1984 Victory tour, Michael sought out Kingdom Halls in whatever cities he played. For years after becoming a star, he would disguise himself and continue to walk door-to-door, as Witnesses are mandated to do, handing out leaflets and proselytizing a theology that he was taught never to question.

And yet question it he did. The questioning, although silent, began early on. When, for instance, the Jacksons moved from Gary, Indiana, to Hollywood at the spectacular start of their recording career, Michael lived for several months with Diana Ross, who, recognizing his ultrasensitive soul, introduced him to the world of art. Together they spent hours leafing through books devoted to the High Renaissance paintings of Michelangelo and to cubist portraits by Pablo Picasso. Instinctually, Michael recognized the sensuousness in religious paintings and the spirituality in secular works. Even as a preteen, he sensed the contradictions and paradoxes in artistic expression. He knew that tension was inherent in drama and that drama was a key ingredient of great art. He learned that art, unlike his mother's religion, could contain confusion.

His private tutor, a gentle Jewish woman named Ruth Fine, had homeschooled him and his brothers, as well as sister Janet, since they were young children. She accompanied them on the road and saw in Michael an active and inquisitive mind. When she spoke of her own religion as she introduced him to works of literature, he listened, and he read carefully, wondering whether, as the Witnesses claimed, all those who failed to adhere to their doctrine — even sweet souls like Miss Fine — would be denied eternal life. That made little sense, and yet Michael couldn't — or wouldn't — confront his mother with his doubts.

As his own artistry grew, he suppressed his doubts. He compartmentalized. Art and music go here; religion and faith go there. He could sing love songs and dance songs and even super-sexy songs on Saturday and still go to the Kingdom Hall on Sunday with a full and pure heart. Nothing could deter him from being his mother's dutiful child.

It was in the eighties at the time of *Thriller* when the compartmentalization ran amok. It was, in fact, the title song that triggered the trauma. Michael's fascination with gothic imagery goes back to his father. He often spoke about how Joseph strapped on a ghoulish Halloween mask and, in the middle of the night, sneaked outside, banged on the bedroom window, and woke up his little boys, scaring them out of their wits. Sometimes, on nights when

Halloween was long past, he actually opened the window and climbed through, and then chased his kids, who thought he was a burglar or a child murderer, all over the house. Although Katherine did not curtail his corporal punishment — even when, as Michael once explained, Joseph stripped his sons of their clothes and covered them in oil before administering the beating — she did object to this frightening form of abuse. And yet Joseph continued. When Michael developed acne as a teenager, Joseph teased him unmercifully. So intense was the antagonism that Michael later confessed to his sister Janet that he fantasized about his father's death and, with pleasure, imagined what it would be like to view him in his coffin.

Death crept into Michael's imagination and remained there until, as a mature artist in his midtwenties, he found a vehicle to vent his anguish. "Thriller" was the first of such vehicles, as both a song and a short film. The story operates on many levels at once. As an all-American guy wearing a letter jacket, Michael is out on a date with sweet sweater girl Ola Ray. Suddenly his car runs out of gas. They are walking alone in the woods when Michael turns into a werewolf and viciously assaults her. But that's only make-believe. We switch perspectives to see that, in Michael's words, "it's only a movie." He and Ola Ray are merely members of an audience watching a horror film that Michael is relishing. When they're leaving the theater, the groove kicks in and the main musical text unfolds. The dead rise from their graves and join in a lavishly choreographed dance, Michael leading the way. The horror has been contained. But not for long. The horror explodes and the living dead pursue Ola Ray. They're on the verge of devouring her when, just like that, Michael wakes her from the dream. The horror was only in her imagination. For a second time, Michael has brought her back to reality. He's no longer a werewolf, no longer a ghoul; he's simply a normal guy on a date with a normal gal. Before the film ends, though, we zoom in on Michael's eyes and see that, after all is said and done, our guy isn't normal at all. He's paranormal. The spooky yellow of his eyes tells you that he is, in fact, an otherworldly character.

This highly complex gothic tale upset the Jehovah's Witnesses. Because Michael still sought their approval—and by extension the approval of his mother—he added this disclaimer to the start of the film:

"Due to my strong personal convictions, I wish to stress that this film in no way endorses a belief in the occult."

Yet a break was inevitable. It came in 1987, with the production of the video for "Smooth Criminal," in which, to save the day, Michael mows down a phalanx of marauders with a machine gun. This was too much for the Witnesses. This time, however, Michael offered neither a qualification nor an apology. The *Los Angeles Times* reported that the Witnesses' Woodland Hills congregation, the Kingdom Hall that Katherine had been attending since moving to California, "disassociated" Michael from its sect. According to church rules, that meant that Michael's mother, who would never abandon her adherence to the faith, was not allowed to discuss the dismissal with her son.

Just as the twenty-one-year-old Michael had disassociated himself from his father, firing him as his manager in 1979, eight years later Michael could no longer look to his mother for theological guidance. Joseph had been dismissed in the secular realm, and Katherine was, in essence, dismissed in the spiritual. As a result, Michael was, in the words of Charles Brown's classic blues, "drifting and drifting, like a ship out on the sea."

On this Sunday in March of 2009, the drifting continues. Michael feels untethered from his parents and his past. He feels uncertain about his future.

To ease his mind, Michael turns to the classical music he has long loved, like Prokofiev's *Peter and the Wolf*, a symphony set to a children's story with a sharp edge of danger and the threat of death, elements that Michael relishes in fables. He listens to Chopin piano sonatas and Beethoven string quartets, wordless creations that shower him with soothing harmonies, comfort him with lush melodies, and awaken him to the geniuses of past eras, to artists he feels certain are channeling the beauty of God.

At heart, Michael remains, in the language of his mother, a God-fearing man. Because God is invisible and inaudible, because God is manifest obliquely through the Holy Scriptures and holy works of art, it was so much easier to understand God when God was so thoroughly explained by the Jehovah's Witnesses.

Since separating from his mother's community of true

believers two decades earlier, he has sat with spiritual uncertainty. Michael is not a biblical scholar. He is not given to reading theology. Yet his love of the Lord is boundless. His feeling that the God of love lives and moves through our lives in a million wondrous ways remains strong as ever, even if there is no society of worshippers to anchor him.

Rabbi Shmuley Boteach, the writer and media personality who drew close to Michael in 2000, concluded that Michael might find greater balance in his life if he could only re-embrace his childhood faith. The rabbi saw him drifting. Katherine saw the same thing. In her conversations with Boteach, she related how she still passed on Jehovah's Witness literature to Grace Rwaramba, longtime nanny to Michael's children. Katherine still hoped to bring her lost boy back into the fold, just as brother Jermaine tried, albeit unsuccessfully, to indoctrinate him into Islam.

Without a community, without a religious ritual, Sunday is a hard day.

Prokofiev helps. Chopin and Beethoven help. It helps to hear the children laughing from the next room. It helps to gather them around him, to feel their love and sweet innocence.

But on Sunday, time moves slowly, and at night, sleep, precious sleep, comes not at all.

6

Managerial Warfare

"The greats are basically unmanageable," Marvin Gaye once said. "I believe it's true of most artists with outsized talent. We're led by our creativity, not by managerial decisions. We can't be controlled or fenced in. I know that's true of me, I know it's true of Stevie Wonder, and from what I've heard, it was true of Mr. Mozart. Wasn't his dad trying to manage him? Well, that makes me think of Michael Jackson, another supertalent and an artist who I'm guessing is going to be unmanageable."

Gaye made the observation in 1980, in the aftermath of the release of Michael's hit album *Off the Wall*. The statement proved prophetic. Over the course of his career, Michael hired and fired at least a dozen managers. A few were hired and fired twice. He had dozens of close advisors, many of whom were billionaires. Because his sweet nature elicited sympathy and his scattered focus revealed vulnerability, he was prey to both the well-intentioned and the unscrupulous. Fabulously wealthy princes like Sheikh

Abdullah, who controlled an oil-rich kingdom, formed partnerships with Michael that seemingly guaranteed his financial security. And yet those partnerships inevitably crumbled, usually resulting in multimillion-dollar lawsuits. He was advised by mentors like Mohamed Al-Fayed, owner of the London department store Harrods, and Prince Al-Waleed bin Talal of Saudi Arabia. Billionaires like Al Malnik, Ron Burkle, and George Maloof allowed Michael and his children to live in luxury, free of charge, until he got back on his feet — and yet that was never enough. Because of his mismanagement, he always needed more — more help, more money, more ways to save himself from going under.

"Michael really had no concept of money," said Walter Yetnikoff, president of CBS Records during the eighties, when he was one of Michael's closest advisors. "At a time when *Thriller* was selling a million copies a week, he felt like he had all the money in the world. He couldn't conceive of his money ever running out. And because his work ethic was so strong — his work ethic had, in fact, been strong since he was a child — he couldn't help but feel entitled. Rightfully so, he felt that he earned all he made. But that meant there was no limit to his spending.

"We all have addictions — mine have become the stuff of legend — but I really do believe that Michael's clearest addiction was to spending. When it came to shelling out money for anything, Michael had no pause button, no control. Spending gave him instant gratification. It made him feel powerful. His spending also applied to things like gifts and charity. No one was more giving. But it also had to do with self-indulgence. He wouldn't think twice about moving into the highest-price hotel anywhere in the world, renting out the top floor, which might mean ten rooms in addition to the royal suite, and staying there for a month. And when it came to production budgets for his music or videos, the sky was the limit. In that case, it wasn't his money — CBS was paying those bills — so his spending was even more outrageous. It meant nothing for Michael to rent out two or three fully staffed studios at the same time, with engineers on call 24/7. If he showed up to work at one of those studios, fine. If he didn't, that was okay too. He just wanted the convenience of being able to work whenever and wherever he wanted. And because he was making a fortune — for us and as well for himself — no one was about to tell him no."

Of Michael's many managers, the one who looms largest is Frank Dileo, a former employee of Yetnikoff's whom Michael came to call Uncle Tookie. Michael hired Dileo in 1984, when *Thriller* was still setting the industry on fire.

"Frank was working for me as a promo man at Epic records," said Yetnikoff. "That's the subsidiary label that had acts like Cyndi Lauper, Culture Club, and Michael. Dileo was the conduit between the label and the independent promotion men. Those were the guys responsible for getting airplay. In the eighties, they were incredibly important to sales success. Some considered the promo men a vestige of the old payola system. From where I stood, as grand czar of CBS Records, I didn't have time to make moral judgments about influencing program directors. The shareholders wanted profits, and that meant I had to deliver hits. No one was better at working the independent promo system than Dileo. He was at the helm of the sales force when, out of the seven singles we released from *Thriller,* all seven went top ten. That had never happened before. I'm not saying Michael's musicianship wasn't absolutely terrific — it was — but Dileo's salesmanship was equally terrific, and Michael knew it. Which is why he asked whether I'd be upset if he hired Frank as his manager.

"I wasn't at all upset. I was delighted. I was glad to have one of my confidants so close to Michael. Besides, I got a kick out of watching the two of them. Frank stood about as tall as a fire hydrant and was easily twice as wide. He always had to have an extra-long, extra-thick cigar sticking out of his mouth. Never met a man with such a strong center of gravity. One time, just for fun, I tried to knock him over. I body-slammed him and wound up on my ass. Frank hadn't moved an inch. I think that's another reason Michael liked him. He saw him as a rock-solid, steadying influence. It didn't matter to Michael any more than it mattered to me that earlier in Frank's career, he'd been convicted for betting on college basketball, a minor offense. More major was his uncanny ability to keep Michael Jackson songs and videos in heavy rotation from one corner of the globe to the other."

When asked about Michael's managers before Dileo, Yetnikoff was less enthusiastic. "In the seventies and early eighties, when he was still with his brothers, his father was in the picture, along with Ron Weisner. But during those years, even when he broke through with *Off the Wall*, he still hadn't come into his own, and management wasn't as crucial as it became with *Thriller*."

"It was during *Thriller* that Michael fired Ron Weisner and had no management at all," Quincy Jones remembered. "This alarmed me. I compared it to a 747 flying around with no one in the cockpit. So when he finally saw the need and hired Dileo, I was relieved."

"When Michael relieved Dileo of all his duties in 1989, if he could have, he would have canned me as well," said Yetnikoff. "The problem was that he had this fixation about *Bad* selling a hundred million copies. At that point, *Thriller* might have sold fifty million, and Michael was determined that *Bad* would have to double that number. The truth is that *Bad* spawned five number one singles. At the time, no other album had ever accomplished that, not even *Thriller*. It didn't matter to Michael that, by any normal measure, *Bad* was a worldwide smash, selling tens of millions. Because he couldn't stop comparing it to *Thriller*, a once-in-a-lifetime phenomenon that would never be matched, he considered *Bad* a failure and started firing the key members of his team — mainly his lawyer, John Branca, and manager, Dileo — who had been so critical to his success. He wanted David Geffen to take over as manager. But Geffen saw himself as a mogul, not a manager. Geffen asked Michael, 'Do you wash windows?' 'No, I don't wash windows,' Michael said. 'Well, I don't manage,' Geffen said. So Michael hired Sandy Gallin, who was also handling Dolly Parton and Cher. That's about the same time — 1990 — I got fired from

Sony, the Japanese firm I convinced to buy CBS Records. My underling, Tommy Mottola, took over. History would prove that Mottola had an even harder time managing Michael than anyone."

The Michael-Mottola relationship imploded in 2001, when Michael claimed that Sony wasn't properly promoting *Invincible*, his new release. He went so far as to hold a press conference, where he was introduced by Reverend Al Sharpton. That's when Michael called Mottola a devilish racist. Mottola argued that Sony had spent some $40 million on the production and promotion of *Invincible*, and that if the record's sales didn't exceed those of *Thriller*—Michael's unchanging goal—it was not the label's fault.

Invincible did reach number one, but its worldwide sales of eight million were seen as a disappointment and evidence of a decided downturn in Michael's commercial appeal. Two thousand and one was also the year of the CBS television special celebrating Michael's thirtieth year in music. The show, which included a Jackson brothers reunion, was taped during two concerts—one on September 7, the other on September 10, the night before the terrorist attacks on the World Trade Center. The national tragedy overwhelmed Michael's big celebration.

Three years later, in the summer of 2004, Michael, charged with seven counts of committing lewd acts against a minor, was viscerally moved to see Frank Dileo, the manager he had fired some fifteen years earlier, seated in the Santa Barbara County courthouse, there to lend his support.

Now, in March of 2009, the question of who manages Michael — a question that has vexed him for the past three decades — is more crucial and confusing than ever.

Michael was raised to do the right thing. From the start, he was the ultimate good boy: obedient, respectful of authority, a model son. But when the role of father merged with the roles of musical coach and business manager, emotional confusion ensued. Young Michael derived great pleasure from thrilling audiences at venues — high school sock hops, shopping center openings, nightclubs, and theaters — that had been booked by his dad. At the same time, he railed against Joseph's tyrannical disposition. Because he sensed his own inordinate talent at an early age, Michael assumed a stance of leadership. Even as a kid, he was the front man. And of all the Jackson boys, Michael took the brunt of Joseph's rage. He literally got hit hardest.

In his memoir, *Moonwalk*, Michael described throwing a shoe at Joseph and swinging at him with his little fists. He claimed that he got abused more than all his brothers combined. When Joseph attacked him, he remembered fighting back, although, in Michael's words, "My father would kill me, just tear me up."

And yet throughout his life, Michael would credit Joseph with teaching him all he knew. Along with bitter resentment, there was heartfelt gratitude. The result was that in all future relationships with managers, Michael would carry the heavy emotional baggage of his childhood. He would see in every future manager shadows of his original paternal manager. Ron Weisner, Frank Dileo, Sandy

Gallin, Tohme Tohme—all were charismatic men of driving ambition. Each shared Michael's dream, which was, in fact, the dream that he shared with Joseph: not simply spectacular success, but a series of endless successes, one necessarily more record-setting than the next. Each successive manager shared the desperate dream of world conquest. To achieve this dream, Michael needed these men, just as he needed his own father. And just as he resented his father and his father's menacing dominance, so too did Michael resent each of his managers. Consequently, as Marvin Gaye had predicted, Michael was, at once, unmanageable and desperate for good management.

With the This Is It concerts close at hand, Michael knows that he needs management more than ever. He is grateful that his current manager, Tohme Tohme, brought him together with the AEG group. Without AEG, he might well have lost everything. And yet Tohme Tohme, and by extension AEG's Randy Phillips, has taken on the role once held by Joseph. They are imposing upon Michael what he begins to see as a cruel and heartless discipline. Ten shows have turned into fifty. And now Michael is hearing Phillips drop hints that he should really cash in and take the show on the road. Eventually it may go around the world. Michael begins seeing this, like so much of his life, spinning out of control.

He grows suspicious of Tohme Tohme. It was Tohme Tohme who first convinced Michael that selling some of the contents of Neverland would rid him of depressing memories and gain him much-needed revenue. When Michael agreed, Tohme Tohme contracted Julien's Auctions to facilitate the sale. In describing the enormous quantity of art up for sale, auctioneer Darren Julien described it as "Disneyland collides with the Louvre."

But when Michael saw the catalog in which photographs of those contents were featured, he had a change of heart. He couldn't stand the idea of losing hundreds of objects dear to him. Eventually the auction was canceled, but the result was still another legal mess. Michael blamed Tohme Tohme.

When other forces sense Tohme Tohme losing favor, they move in for the kill.

Patrick Allocco, head of AllGood, the concert promotion firm, has met with Michael's father in hopes of arranging a Jacksons reunion concert. Joseph allegedly tells Allocco that Frank Dileo is back in Michael's good graces and is the one to facilitate the deal. But later still, another man claims that he's managing Michael: Leonard Rowe, the African American promoter who has also teamed up with Joseph and signed all the Jackson boys minus Michael to a reunion show of his own making. All this is happening before, during, and after Tohme Tohme has gotten Michael to agree to AEG's multiconcert deal.

Millions are at stake.

Millions have been promised.

Given the precarious finances of the Jacksons, whose history is marked by many bankruptcies, Michael's family is eager to get back in the game. The family needs money.

Many of the siblings have not been able to stay afloat for long without Michael's help. The same applies to Joseph. Michael's posttrial refusal to perform or tour — his retreat to Bahrain and Ireland, his seclusion in Vegas — was disastrous for his family's finances. The minute it became clear that Michael might take the stage again, the family — and promoters claiming to represent them — came running.

On March 17, 2009, as Michael prepares to return to the office of Dr. Arnold Klein for more dermatological treatments and more Demerol, the battle for Michael's divided heart and troubled soul is growing uglier, day by day.

7

Spring

Friday, March 20, 2009

Still haunted by insomnia, Michael awakens late in the morning and, before anything else, checks in with his children, who are quietly reading books and playing games. He feels pride when he sees how self-sufficient they have become. Though he dotes on them shamelessly, he has also raised them to follow their natural curiosity. He is determined that, in contrast with his own childhood, in which leisure didn't exist and curiosity about anything other than ways to improve the stage show was never encouraged, Prince, Paris, and Blanket have a freedom never afforded him — the freedom to simply be children. Given the bizarre circumstances of their lives, Michael is especially pleased that they appear well-adjusted and happy.

Although he has never failed to keep them close to him, he has also, particularly in these past six years, led an unsettled and madly peripatetic existence, running from country to country, often covering the children in masks and himself in disguises. In some ways, the unorthodox lifestyle and unpredictable movement may contribute to the bond between Michael and his kids. In Arabian palaces, country estates in Ireland, penthouse hotel suites in Vegas, and now a mansion in Holmby Hills, they huddle together for emotional warmth and the reassurance that, though their world may be ever-shifting and uncertain, they will always have one another. As a family unit, they are extraordinarily tight-knit.

While eating lunch with the kids, Michael hears a TV newscaster announcing that spring has officially arrived. He smiles and sighs, thinking back over these difficult past months. Today there is reason for celebration. Michael sees spring as the season of hope. Spring is victory over the harshness of winter. Spring is about eternal renewal. Jesus came back to life in spring. Spring proves that depression — depression of growth, depression of spirit — is but a temporary thing. Ultimately, depression lifts and we move forward, onward, upward. Looking back, Michael recognizes this as the movement of his life. No matter how deep the misery, he has always managed to overcome. Tenacity is in his blood. Tenacity is in his history. So on this first day of spring, his heart swells with good feeling. He's optimistic. He has faith.

As is often the case when his mood is joyful, he puts on music. Music — especially classical music — heightens his joy. Debussy's Arabesque no. 1 is a piano composition he has heard a thousand times. Each listening brings him enormous pleasure. Waves of sound wash over him, calm him, excite his imagination. He listens to other compositions he has heard hundreds of times before, pieces that invoke a sense of wonderment and delight—Tchaikovsky's *Nutcracker* Suite, Stravinsky's *The Rite of Spring*—and bring him into a world where rejuvenation and replenishment recur in accordance with God's divine plan.

As always, music nourishes Michael. Even the thought of creativity fills him with positive energy. He acts on that energy by going to work on a suite of classical songs that have been stirring his mind for months. Sometimes he hears this music as a theme to an unseen movie, like the film scores of Elmer Bernstein. Among Bernstein's work, his score for *To Kill a Mockingbird* is Michael's favorite. Because it's a story seen from a child's point of view, a film with clear heroes and villains, Michael embraces it with his whole heart. He also identifies closely with the film because it is set in the thirties in small-town Alabama, the very state and moment in time in which Michael's mother grew up.

As the music to some unwritten film swirls around in his head, Michael sings bits of melody and harmony into a tape recorder. For months now, he's been composing what he calls classical music. His plan is to engage an orchestrator to transcribe his work. Because he is unable to read or write music, he depends upon others for his musical notations. Many of his orchestral predecessors— Barry White, Isaac Hayes, Marvin Gaye—were similarly situated. Their musical minds were vast. They conceived enormous melodic and harmonic constructions. In their heads, they could hear the completed piece. They were able to delineate each discrete part, from the strings to the brass to the reeds to the rhythm. Like Michael, they were musically preliterate. Their lack of formal training, though, in no way impeded their ability to forge compositions of great beauty and deep complexity.

Michael's musical reveries don't last long. His serene mood is shattered when he is reminded of an ugly press report. For his entire adult life, he has had a troubled relationship with publicity.

Early on, he understood its essential role in show business. He saw how, although Bobby Taylor brought the Jackson 5 to Motown, the label changed the story, telling the world it was Diana Ross who discovered the group. Taylor remembered how Michael came to him and said, "It isn't true, Bobby. You were the one who found us. Now they want us to lie."

"This was an innocent kid," said Taylor, "with a pure heart. I hated to break it to him, but I had no choice. 'Look, Mike,' I said, 'this is how this mean ol' world works. To attract the maximum amount of attention, sometimes you have to make up things. If you don't, there's a good chance you'll be ignored. And being ignored in this business is the kiss of death.'"

A couple of years later, when *Rolling Stone* put Michael on the cover with the heading "Why does this eleven-year-old stay up past his bedtime?" the truth was that Michael was almost thirteen. By then, though, exaggerating his youth was nothing new. His father had been doing it for years. The thrill of seeing himself on a magazine cover compensated for the distorted facts. Besides, what harm was done?

The harm came in the eighties. Michael had long been accustomed to the limelight, but the onslaught of super-stardom overheated the engines of his already burning ambition. Bob Jones, head of Motown publicity, had worked with the Jacksons since 1970, and in the mideighties was hired by Michael as his personal publicist. Though Jones was unceremoniously dismissed in 2004, when called to testify in the 2005 trial, he was protective of his former employer.

"When it came to publicity," Bob Jones once explained, "Michael was a mad genius. In that heady period between *Thriller* and *Bad*, he found it difficult to process the enormity of his success. While it's true that he'd been a star since he was a little kid, he suddenly found himself in an entirely different position — this wildly exalted position — and he just wasn't prepared. Being the world's biggest star — bigger than even the Hollywood stars he idolized, like Gregory Peck, Katharine Hepburn, Sophia Loren, Fred Astaire, and Elizabeth Taylor — excited him tremendously. You have to remember that this was when the company he admired most, Disney, was begging him to create a movie for their amusement parks, and just like that, he found himself in discussions with George Lucas and Steven Spielberg. All this sent him over the top.

"He was absolutely thrilled by this avalanche of publicity. Like every entertainer I've ever known, he loved being on the cover of dozens of magazines. He reveled in all the attention. And he also couldn't get enough. Because the press was so solicitous, so eager to grab any crumb he threw their way, he began to toy with them. Many of those absurd stories, like the one about his sleeping in a hyperbaric chamber, originated from him. He had me leak those items and got a good laugh when they actually appeared in print.

"Part of this has to do with Michael's playfulness: he likes to scare guests with Muscles, his boa constrictor. He never tires of dropping water balloons on unsuspecting victims and engaging in water gun fights. I warned him, though, that playing with the press is risky business. Today they love you. Tomorrow they devour you. But those were days when Michael truly felt invincible. As naive as it sounds, he really did believe that he could go on managing the press, just the way he managed the making of his music. When this strategy blew up in his face, when, in the early nineties, the accusations assaulted him and the media turned on him with a vengeance, his rage, I believe, was not only directed at the press, but also directed at himself for creating a dangerous dynamic that had spun so crazily out of control."

Many of Michael's most emotionally charged and lyrically engaged songs — "Leave Me Alone," "Why You Wanna Trip on Me," "Scream," "Tabloid Junkie," "Privacy," and the posthumously released "Price of Fame" and "Breaking News" — center on what became his poisonous relationship with the press.

"Part of the problem," said Bob Jones, "was that Michael identified with historical figures like Howard Hughes and

P. T. Barnum. He told me that he loved Hughes because of Hughes's uncanny ability to intrigue the public. He loved how Hughes was able to play people. Michael also had me buy copies of Barnum's biography *Humbug* for everyone at MJJ Productions. It was required reading. Michael loved how Barnum created spectacle, but he also loved how he created illusion. But mainly he admired how Barnum had the press eating out of his hand. When it came to putting on the greatest show on earth, anything goes. That was Michael's philosophy. The trouble, of course, was that Barnum was working in the nineteenth century. In the twentieth century of Michael Jackson, the press didn't mind biting the hand that fed it. Soon as they drew blood, feeding frenzies ensued. That blood sport became a major industry unto itself. And the more Michael tried to derail the industry, the more he cried out against it, the stronger it became."

On this Friday in March, Michael is reading reports on the latest attacks against him. Earlier in the month, two British soldiers had been allegedly killed by the Irish Republican Army, the military force that had been powerful in the eighties. Two English comics commented on television that they weren't sure which phenomenon from the eighties they wanted back less: the IRA or Michael Jackson.

Michael is shocked. He's being compared to a murderous militia. The analogy makes his blood run cold. Why would anyone make such an insinuation, even as a joke?

Why would anyone go out of his way to say something so deeply hurtful?

Michael is crestfallen. He begins to worry that public opinion in England is turning against him. Compared with the United States, where he had been doggedly prosecuted, England is supposedly safe ground. His attraction to the O_2 Arena as a comeback venue was largely about its location. He felt that England and Europe were far more forgiving than his home country. But now he remembers that it was in England that the "Wacko Jacko" moniker began. He forgets that he has contributed to this picture of himself as an oddity. Even four years after his acquittal on every charge leveled against him, he feels that he still stands accused. When will the accusations stop? When will the media have its fill of finding fault? When will it stop looking for ways to wound him?

Michael has long fought the feeling of being a victim. He has read enough psychology and self-help tomes to know that victimhood is an emotional trap. Once we start to feel persecuted by the world, the world turns dark. Doom envelops us. It's imperative that we *not* see ourselves as victims. We're in control of our own mental states. We can be whoever we want to be. We can stay positive, ignore the nastiness, and make progress. Michael is determined to move forward.

At the same time, Michael cannot easily break a pattern established early in his career. He cannot pretend not to care what the world thinks of him. He is, after all, an entertainer. Entertainers live on the love of their fans. And if Michael's fans are fed lies, if they are led to believe that he is, in the insinuation of the English comics, as villainous as a killer, doesn't he have every right to be upset? Isn't he entitled to express the pain that such comparisons bring? Is he supposed to simply sit back and take it?

No. He instructs his people to issue a statement that says, "Michael was told about the comments and was appalled. It was a disgusting slur. To compare him to cold-blooded murderers is not funny. It's highly offensive."

Michael feels crushed. He feels that, even on this first day of spring, even at a time when renewal is in the air and optimism should prevail, avoiding cynicism isn't easy. No matter how valiantly Michael tries to present a wholly positive agenda, the press will never tire of slandering him. He despairs at the thought that he is powerless in this unending war.

8

Father, Father

In *What's Going On,* the sublime suite of songs released in 1971 — the same year the Jackson 5 hit with "Never Can Say Goodbye," and their Saturday morning cartoon show debuted on ABC — Marvin Gaye sang about crying mothers and dying brothers. He also invoked the image of his own father when he exclaimed, "Father, father, we don't need to escalate." Gaye was referring to both the Vietnam War and the personal war he had waged with his father ever since the singer, like Michael, had suffered beatings as a small child. The brutal battle between father and son was a lifetime preoccupation for Marvin Gaye and Michael Jackson alike.

Like Marvin, Michael put Mother on a pedestal, despite the fact, that in both cases, Mother was unable to protect her son from her husband's violence. Like Marvin, Michael worked hard to transcend the hostility. He knew that holding hatred in his heart damaged his soul. When Marvin was murdered by his father on April 1, 1984, Michael, at the height of his *Thriller* success, was grappling with the Victory tour. He yielded to pressure from his mother, even though he had no interest in reuniting with his brothers, knowing that the tour would also involve his father — something that Michael desperately wanted to avoid. That troubled father-son relationship, as much as he tried to escape it, would haunt him for the rest of his life.

"If my mother had only thrown my father out of the house and once and for all divorced the man," Gaye once said, "my life would be easier. If she could get rid of him, maybe I'd be able to do the same."

These words could have been spoken by Michael, whose mother, despite the knowledge that Joseph fathered a child with another woman in 1974, would never divorce her husband. Though they have maintained separate residences for years, Katherine's permanent attachment to Joseph meant that Michael would be bound to Joseph as well, no matter how frantically he tried to distance himself. To be in a relationship with Mother necessitated being in a relationship with Father. The triangulation — Katherine, Joseph, Michael — would hold firm for the duration.

The week of Monday, March 23, 2009, begins with Michael worrying about his mother's repeated requests that he meet with his father and Leonard Rowe. It was, in fact, Joseph who first hired Rowe back in the late seventies to book a Jacksons tour.

Joseph wants back into his son's business. Backed by

Patrick Allocco, head of AllGood Entertainment, Rowe is assuring Joseph that there are millions to be made. Better yet, those millions can be made from a single concert, not fifty.

Distressed, Michael sees how the opposing forces are lining up:

Joseph, Katherine, Rowe, and Allocco stand on one side of the divide.

AEG's Randy Phillips and Michael's manager, Tohme Tohme, stand on the other.

In a perfect world—in Michael's idealized world— reconciliation is realized. Everyone works together for the greater good. Thus he avoids the emotional situation he likes the least: a confrontation. He longs for peace, not merely among the warring factions but inside his soul. He is battle-weary. At the same time, he feels himself drawn to both camps.

Tohme Tohme did negotiate the AEG plan, which has allowed him to keep his half of the vast Sony/ATV music catalog and his many assets, including Neverland. Only the AEG plan has provided a strategy for buying Prince Jefri's sprawling Las Vegas estate. There is also a proviso for a multimillion-dollar development deal to produce a movie version of "Thriller," with Michael locked in as producer.

For good reasons, he trusts Tohme Tohme.

But for other good reasons, he does not.

Michael is still upset that Tohme Tohme lacked the sensitivity to realize that auctioning items from Neverland—and publishing photos of those items in a splashy public catalog—would bring him embarrassment and pain. And wasn't it Tohme Tohme who conspired with AEG to increase the This Is It concert count from ten to thirty to fifty?

If he was really protecting me, Michael wonders, *wouldn't he have found a better solution than piling on to an already overbearing workload?*

Then there is the simple fact that Michael loves his mother dearly. He would like for her to personally profit from his return to the stage. He would also like to please her by trying—as he has tried countless times in the past—to reconcile with his father, just as she has always been able to reconcile with her husband. If that means meeting Joseph and Leonard Rowe simply to hear them out, well, isn't that the least he can do for the woman he treasures above all others?

He fears that his father, known to express hostility and skepticism toward white agents and promoters, will surely express that same view about white-owned AEG. In 1983, Michael felt moved to publicly respond to what were perceived as Joseph's racist remarks concerning the Jacksons' white managers, Ron Weisner and Freddy DeMann. "To hear him talk that way turns my stomach," said Michael, referring to his father's comments about the "white help." Michael added, "Racism is not my motto."

As former president of the Black Promoters Association, Leonard Rowe has long complained about racial prejudice in the record industry. And of course Michael himself protested against bigotry in the music business when he publicly lashed out against Sony after the release of his last studio album, *Invincible*, in 2001. In taking that stance, he found himself saying some of the same words he had heard his father speak.

And why not? Isn't his father a strong and fearless man who quit the steel mill and, against odds of a million to one, whipped his sons into shape and turned them into professionals with enough polish and pizzazz to win over the world? Isn't Joseph a model — maybe *the* ultimate model — for taking on the phonies and the manipulators? Isn't he a stand-up guy who never fails to stand up for himself and his family? Joseph has never backed down or broken down. He has what it takes to get through the thorniest situations. He has real guts. And, best of all, he never falls apart.

Falling apart is a real fear for Michael. In agreeing to this strenuous schedule in London, he continually worries about whether there will be enough time to mount the spectacular shows he envisions, and whether he has the stamina required to endure the ordeal.

As Michael's worries mount, so does his desire to return to his dermatologist, Dr. Arnold Klein. On this same Monday in March, Michael's usual entourage of two blue Escalades carries him to Beverly Hills, where Klein gives him two hundred milligrams of Demerol so he can tolerate the pain of Botox injections under the eyes. Michael's antiaging obsession is as great as ever. In the artist's Peter Pan pursuit of staying forever young, Klein is his main ally. In the next fourteen weeks, Michael will spend nearly $50,000 on dermatological treatments.

He is preoccupied with his face—the face that suffered from endless outbreaks of acne and was the subject of vicious teasing when he was a boy; the face that he considered repugnant; the face that, the minute Michael had the means, was resculpted into a form that, to his eyes, was flawless. A face that, in short, bore no resemblance to the face of his father.

And yet he can't stop seeing his father's face as he struggles to decide whether to meet him and Leonard Rowe at Carolwood estate.

It has been years since he faced his father, years since he has even spoken to him on the phone. He has needed that time away. Michael has needed to avoid Joseph's incessant and aggressive pressure to engage his son in one deal or another. Yet Michael also yearns for some rapprochement. He wants to forgive.

For a couple of years beginning in 2000, when Rabbi Shmuley Boteach became Michael's spiritual guru, one of the rabbi's essential directives was that Michael forgive his father. At the time, Michael was living in New York and working on *Invincible*. Always looking for normalcy in family life—hence his long-term relationship with the Cascios of New Jersey—Michael loved sharing home-cooked Friday night dinners with the rabbi's family to celebrate the Jewish Sabbath. It was the rabbi who arranged for Michael to address England's Oxford University in

March of 2001 and promote the artist's Heal the Kids charity and children's universal bill of rights.

Cynics saw this as part of Michael's campaign to rehabilitate himself in the public eye. But it's difficult to read Michael's remarks, especially those concerning his father, and doubt his sincerity.

Michael speaks with great empathy about his father's long days in the steel mill doing work that "kills the lungs and humbles the spirit." It's no wonder, he claims, that Joseph had trouble expressing his emotions, no wonder he developed a hardened heart. Now, through forgiving eyes, Michael sees Joseph's "harshness" as a "kind of love." He now understands that his father pushed him because he loved him. He says that in the place of bitterness toward his father he feels a blessing; instead of anger he has found "absolution." Reconciliation has replaced revenge. And what used to be fury has turned into forgiveness.

It's a beautiful speech, and yet those feelings, no matter how genuine, were not enough to forge a lasting bond or even renew the fragile father-son relationship. While Joseph did stand by his son's side during the grueling trial in 2005, once the acquittal came and Michael fled the country, the son cut off all contact with the father, returning to the pattern he had established in the eighties. The less Michael saw of Joseph — and the less Joseph became entangled in Michael's business — the better.

And yet now, on March 23, 2009, Michael is unhappy. He feels boxed in by a manager, Tohme Tohme, whom he has known for little more than a year. He feels constrained by the contractual complexities engineered by AEG and wonders if he's being manipulated. Adding further to his distress is the distress of his mother. She won't be satisfied until, after all these years, he agrees to see his father and his father's friend—a man whom Katherine considers a friend of all the Jacksons—Leonard Rowe.

After days of agonizing over the decision, he makes up his mind.

In the name of reconciliation and forgiveness, in the name of family solidarity and family trust, he agrees to let Joseph and Rowe come to the house the day after tomorrow.

He knows his mother will be happy and his father will be excited. He knows that Leonard Rowe, a man he likes, will try with all his might to reassert himself in Michael's affairs. He knows he may be making a mistake, but he's thought about this long enough—and he'd rather be making music. Michael would always rather be making music.

In addition to the classical pieces that he's been composing, Michael has never stopped writing pop songs, soul songs, rock songs—all songs geared to give free rein to the voices chattering inside his head.

In Michael's personal life, these truculent and demanding voices are in continual conflict and are the source of confusion and pain. One voice, for instance, tells him to avoid his father, while another voice tells him to embrace him. One voice says to rid himself of Tohme Tohme and have outside advisors scrutinize his deal with AEG, while another voice says to leave well enough alone.

In Michael's musical life, though, he is able to blend these various voices. Conflict and confusion are harmonized into melodies of beauteous consolation. So he runs to music like a believer runs to church. Music is his strength and salvation.

In "Keep Your Head Up," for example, a song he recently wrote with Eddie Cascio — the son of his dear New Jersey friend Dominic Cascio and a young man he has known since he was a small boy — Michael works in the style of painter Edward Hopper, whose portraits of lonely and isolated figures in the landscape of Depression-era America reveal the naked souls of his subjects. Michael's subject in "Keep Your Head Up" is a single mother working two jobs, a woman beaten down by life. He offers her both empathy and hope. Then, in the tradition of Marvin Gaye's *What's Going On*, the personal is extended to the eco-political. The song's subject expands beyond the lonely woman looking for sustenance. Mankind is indicted for "sucking up the air" and scarring "the earth from under me." For all the environmental ruin, the singer can hardly breathe and see beyond the blight. And yet it is hope generated by love that informs the song and situates it as another of Michael's sacred anthems. "Keep Your Head Up," like countless other Michael Jackson compositions, is recorded but remains unreleased during his lifetime.

His storehouse of material is Michael's refuge from the

storm. There are pure songs of extravagant multipart harmony in which seemingly every voice inside Michael's head is lovingly merged into lush melodies. "(I Like) The Way You Love Me" is one such song. There are others, like "Monster" and "Threatened," that allow Michael to return to gothic horror, tales in which "everywhere you seem to turn" terror stares you in the face. For Michael, though, the terror also takes the form of the press. It's the paparazzi, he cries, that's the monster. He calls out the entire Hollywood culture. Hollywood itself, with its unyielding insistence on bodily perfection and its insatiable appetite for scurrilous gossip, is the grossest monster of all.

In "Hollywood Tonight," another tale of desperation, the character in question is a fifteen-year-old girl, a runaway bound for the glories of Hollywood, her head filled with dreams of stardom, her name changed so that she, like Michael—the man who is imagining her to life—might reinvent herself and put the pain of her past behind her.

Michael is further comforted and distracted by the brilliance of a song written and recorded years earlier with rocker Lenny Kravitz. Michael adopts the story as his own, especially at this time and in this place. The title says "(I Can't Make It) Another Day." The theme is clear: only the other will save the singer from despair and self-destruction. But there's no telling if the other is a mystical deity or the object of earthly romance. The recurring motif, the message that resonates in Michael's heart, speaks to the search—the endless quest for redemptive love. Even as he leans in and, over Kravitz's brilliant track, continues to sing

"I can't make it another day," Michael is, in fact, suggesting just the opposite: he's triumphing over despondency by allowing music to let him make it through another day.

And even though the day is good, even though he has found solace in making sounds and crafting stories, when night arrives the doubts return. Uncertainty plagues him, and as usual, he struggles to find the peaceful rest he so deeply desires.

9

Managing Managers

On March 25, 2009, nearly four years after Michael left the country with his children following his dramatic acquittal, he is finally prepared — or unprepared — to allow his father back into his life. Until now, he has refused to see him or even speak to him on the phone.

The last time Joseph tried to see his son was two years earlier, when Michael and the children were living in a rented estate in Vegas. Michael's brother Randy, who had managed him at the time of the 2005 trial, had also attempted to gain entrance. At different times, both father and sibling were turned away. Both became enraged. Joseph berated the security guys, claiming that they wouldn't have their jobs — there would be no Michael Jackson — were it not for him. Randy grew so furious that he rammed his car into the gate. That happened on the night of Elizabeth Taylor's seventy-fifth birthday party. Michael was so upset by the incident that he canceled plans to attend the celebration. Yet he still didn't let Randy in. He knew what his brother and father wanted—money, money, and more money—and he was not prepared to engage them in any discussion concerning his business.

But there was another reason for turning them away, a more complex one: Michael feared that if he did entertain their concerns, he would give in to their demands. In short, Michael didn't trust himself. He dreaded confrontations, and rather than fight, he was conditioned to surrender. Pleasing people was second nature to him. That's why, when faced with people he did not wish to please—people he distrusted—avoidance was his default strategy.

On this last Wednesday in March, though, he is no longer able to implement avoidance. Out of respect for his mother and in an attempt to gain clarity over his relationship with Tohme Tohme and AEG, Michael is allowing Joseph and Leonard Rowe into the Carolwood estate.

Michael is right to be concerned about his propensity to placate strong-minded men. As he faces his father—his original manager—and Leonard Rowe, a promoter he knows well, the result of the meeting is predictable.

Michael submits.

The next day Rowe issues a press release that states, "Michael Jackson, universally acclaimed as the King of Pop, today named Leonard Rowe, the legendary concert promoter from Atlanta, as his new manager, replacing Dr. Tohme Tohme."

Michael is quoted as saying, "I am very pleased that Leonard has accepted my offer to manage my business affairs during this important period in my career... Leonard Rowe has been a longtime friend and business associate whose judgment I have come to trust."

Rowe will also produce a letter that Michael promises to sign at a later date. Coming from Michael to Randy Phillips of AEG, the document states the same basic points as the press release. The tremendous power and pull of the original triangulation — father-mother-Michael — has resulted in a coup. Michael is back in the family fold.

But is he?

Some thirty years after firing Joseph as his manager, is Michael now really prepared to grant Joseph, and Joseph's surrogate, control over his comeback?

Rather than taking on these two heavyweights, does he simply choose the path of least resistance? Is he looking only to appease them and then shoo them out of his house as soon as possible?

Or is Michael playing them as he has played so many managers, agents, promoters, and lawyers for so many years?

Or, conversely, are the managers, agents, promoters, and lawyers playing Michael?

The game of who's controlling whom has been going on since Michael first stepped onstage as a small child. It has never stopped. Michael is convinced that it never will.

So let Joseph and Rowe have their victory today. Let them write their press release. Let them rejoice. Let them believe that they have convinced this easily persuaded superstar that they and they alone have his best interests at heart.

In the coming days, though, let them try to call Michael and see if they can get through.

They can't.

Just days after the meeting, Michael no longer has any interest in talking to Rowe, supposedly his new manager.

To make matters even more confusing — a state of affairs that may bring Michael some perverse satisfaction — AllGood Entertainment, the money behind Rowe, is sending a cease and desist notice to AEG. Its claim is that the This Is It shows must be canceled because they are in conflict with a reunion concert to which Michael has agreed.

Uncertain that Rowe has completely solidified his relationship with Michael, AEG is also working with Frank Dileo, Michael's manager from the eighties. Seeing that Tohme Tohme has lost his grip, Dileo is lurking on the sidelines, trading on his once-total access to Michael and assuring both sides — AllGood, with its plans for a reunion, and AEG, with its plans for fifty London concerts — that he has Michael's ear.

Michael is sentimental. His sentimentality complicates things even more. He considers reestablishing ties with former advisors like Dileo and lawyer John Branca. He thinks back fondly on the salad days, the time when *Thriller* and *Bad* were breaking records and money was raining down like manna from heaven. Those were the times when, in Michael's mind, Dileo and Branca could do no wrong.

Michael sees this large cast of characters bumping into one another in a play whose plot is muddled and whose direction is unsure. Sometimes he imagines the play as comic, sometimes tragic. In either case, he must reassert himself as both author and director. It is his story and no one else's.

If today he is willing to entertain Joseph and Rowe, that's fine. If tomorrow he changes course and decides that his decision was hasty, that's his prerogative. If he wants to keep his current manager, Tohme Tohme, he'll keep him. Or if he wants to bring back his old manager Frank Dileo, well, that's his right.

He won't be pinned down.

Such enormous decisions with such huge financial repercussions would require a CEO with long experience in the Wall Street world of high finance. Michael is far from being that person. He is instead a creative artist who lives life emotionally. More than ever, he is ruled by his feelings.

And at the end of March, his feelings are such that he's content to allow his decisions to waver, taking one stance today and retreating from that same stance tomorrow.

Let the factions fight over him however they please. Let them vow loyalty. Let them each claim that they have only his best interests at heart.

Michael has been swimming with showbiz sharks for so long that he is well aware of the dangers. He trusts none of them, yet he needs all of them — or at least at times he believes he does.

Time and again, he has made a mess of his financial life. Having earned tens of millions, he has spent tens of millions more than he has made.

He needs money. He loves what money can buy. But as

someone raised as a fundamentalist Christian, he's persuaded that money really *is* the root of all evil. He sees what it's done to his family. He sees what it's done to him.

Art, uncorrupted by money, calls to him.

The pure act of creativity is the one distraction that saves his sanity. In that act, managers and mothers, fathers and agents, lawyers and promoters, play no part.

The song he hears inside his head is "Leave Me Alone," the plaintive cry from the *Bad* album in which he asks the world to stop dogging him, stop deceiving him, stop making him feel sorry. This is the song in which he tells the world not to come begging at his doorstep.

Another song he hears inside his head is "Unbreakable," from the *Invincible* album, in which he wonders why so many presume that they can get to him with any scheme, and why others seek to bury him. This is the song in which he confirms his tenacity. He won't be stopped.

He'll live with the confusion. He'll deal with what he has to deal with, but he'll escape. "Xscape," the unreleased song that Michael wrote a decade earlier with producer Rodney Jerkins, has him lamenting a pernicious system controlling his life. He needs to find an exit, a way to escape so he can free his mind. The system — the malicious press, the incestuous network of moguls, managers, and agents — is ruling the world. The system is ruling *his* world. The system will surely bring him down if he doesn't find the strength to persevere. He views the system as an omnipotent author intent on writing endless lies. The system is invading his personal space. The system perpetuates a game that he can never win yet cannot afford to lose. The system involves his family, his advisors, his so-called friends. The system is all-pervasive. In singing a song about the system, Michael finds that the act releases the tension. But after the song is sung, the system remains in place. The system is immutable.

Night after night, with thoughts of the system swimming through his brain, Michael cannot sleep.

10

More and Better

At the end of March, with Michael's managerial situation more befuddled than ever, one thing is clear: what counts most is not only pleasing the public but thrilling them. When all is said and done, this has been Michael's primal motive from the very beginning. The emotional chaos surrounding him — the brutality of his father, the maneuvers of his mother, the jealousy of his brothers, the gnawing self-doubt that he developed as a boy — was overwhelmed by the joy of performance. As a performer, he thrived on adulation. Like any normal person, he loved being adored. And even when the adoration became abnormal — when millions of fans throughout the world treated him with worshipful reverence — he sought more. More became his mantra: more record sales, more ticket sales, more recognition from his peers, more awards for his feats, more love from his public.

In Michael's mind, this love is far from unconditional. The love is dependent on giving his fans a better record, a better show, a better performance, than they have ever experienced. He can never rest on his laurels or past triumphs. To do so would invite creative death. Creative life requires a colossal effort to mount a spectacle the likes of which the world has never seen. Relaxation is not an option. The pressure of performance means that mind, body, and spirit are geared to one purpose: the realization of the greatest show on earth. Michael looks to his idols, P. T. Barnum and Walt Disney, and recognizes in them his own relentless drive to attract an ever-wider mass of people into a wondrous world of his own making.

But if This Is It is to succeed—and it must—Michael has no time to lose. That wondrous world requires meticulous planning. Because he demands both absolute perfection and dazzling wizardry, the work ahead is daunting. Michael feels himself swinging into action. It's a good feeling. He beats back the lethargy of these last days, remembering that he's about to assume a role he relishes like no other. He's about to reintroduce himself to the world as one of history's greatest showmen.

He assembles the team that has served him well in the past: director Kenny Ortega, who collaborated with Michael on the Bad and Dangerous tours; Travis Payne, the brilliant choreographer of the "Scream" video; Christian Audigier, the wardrobe coordinator who understands Michael's demand for sartorial sensationalism and is already designing outfits adorned by hundreds of thousands of Swarovski crystals; and band members that include drummer "Sugarfoot" Moffett, young Australian rock guitar virtuoso

Orianthi Panagaris, and singer Judith Hill, who will duet with Michael on the crowd-pleasing "I Just Can't Stop Loving You."

As he lays out his plans to Ortega, it becomes clear that Michael's vision is, as always, for more and better. Beyond the songs themselves — the dozens of his megahits that must be refashioned to appear fresh and new — there is the grand concept. Since the Bad tour in 1988 that concluded with the self-reflective "Man in the Mirror," Michael has sought to give his shows thematic depth. They must be more than the sum of their parts. They must have meaning. In the nineties, Dangerous included "Heal the World," just as HIStory included "Earth Song." Expanding the ecological message, he wants This Is It to hammer home the urgency of the issues surrounding global warming and environmental neglect. Just as he urged his fans to save the children in 1985's "We Are the World" video, twenty-four years later he will implore us to save the planet.

In Michael's view, his high-minded purpose — to raise the consciousness of his audience — must be realized without concern for cost. The visual effects must be the latest and greatest. He wants to employ a helicopter to shoot spectacular angles of Victoria Falls through an IMAX lens. He envisions performing in front of a background of jaw-dropping 3-D videos of himself on the biggest LED screen the world has ever seen. There will be dazzling holograms and an enthralling mash-up of live interactions with filmed images geared to generate shock and awe.

Mounting the stage is a monumental task that must be

accomplished in a matter of weeks. For rehearsals, AEG has rented the soundstages where MGM created the illusion of the burning of Atlanta for the epic film *Gone with the Wind*. Michael relishes his reconnection with Hollywood. He thinks back to those exciting times when, in the eighties, he was working with the most powerful names in show business — Disney, Lucas, Coppola — and made *Captain EO*, a creation that then boasted the biggest budget of any short film in movie history.

Michael demands that AEG fly in not dozens but hundreds of dancers from locations all over the world. He insists that the pool of prospects be vast so that he and Travis Payne can select the best of the best.

It's time to take care of business. Time to start rehearsing. Time to get in shape.

Keeping up the routine he already established, Lou Ferrigno arrives at the Carolwood mansion to find a cheerful Michael playing hide-and-seek with his kids. Later, Lou will describe Michael as the ultimate Mr. Mom.

Dressed in all-black workout attire, Michael is ready to go. For a short while, he and Lou reminisce about the days before the HIStory tour, when the trainer successfully whipped Michael into shape. It will happen again. Lou sees Michael as loose and relaxed, a fun-loving, cooperative client willing to do exercises geared toward building his stamina and maximizing his flexibility.

Still in an ebullient mood after his workout, Michael decides to spend the evening watching movies with the kids — his favorite way to relax. There's *E.T.*, which he's seen a hundred times and of which he narrated a Grammy-winning audio version for children. No character means more to Michael than this pure-hearted alien, misunderstood because of his peculiar form. Children naturally gravitate to E.T. because, in Michael's view, children are trusting. Adults fear E.T. because adults are intolerant.

That night, after Michael puts the kids to bed and kisses them good night, *E.T.* stays on his mind, and he decides to rewatch a film that excites his imagination in a similar fashion: *The Elephant Man.* The story, set in Victorian London, contains all the elements that Michael finds compelling. John Merrick, the central character, is trapped in the kind of freak show that might have been promoted by P. T. Barnum. When walking through the city, Merrick hides his head with a hood. He must conceal his disfigured skull, just as Michael has been moved to disguise his identity when he goes out in public. Merrick appears to be monstrous, but a physician's loving care awakens his mind and brings out the dignity of his character. When cruel sensation-seekers assault him, he cries out, "I am not an animal! I am a human being! I am a man!" Michael relates wholeheartedly. Just as the sensation-seekers torture Merrick, the media tortures Michael. And for all his attempts to reconfigure his face, Michael, like Merrick, has been repelled by his own image for as long as he can remember. Thus he wears masks. Thus he transforms himself into a werewolf. Thus, in the short film he wrote with Stephen King in 1996 called *Ghosts*, Michael plays both the tortured and the torturer, the accused and the accuser, morphing into a variety of different monsters. In the video for "Black or White," a song that pleads the case for tolerance, the morphing takes on epic proportions. Michael's face becomes everyone's face: every race, every hue, every age, every gender.

Michael sees how the world hates the other, the outlier, the one who dares to be different, the disfigured, the alien, the mysterious creature who doesn't speak the language of those who resort to ridicule and scorn.

These are the figures—with their distorted faces and frightening apparitions—to whom Michael passionately relates. He feels for them. He *is* them.

Yet at the same time, as much as he loves how films like *The Elephant Man* challenge our sense of aesthetics, he equally adores fluffy fantasies like *Funny Face,* in which Fred Astaire and Audrey Hepburn scale the heights of song and dance make-believe beauty. Hollywood-defined beauty—especially in the picture-perfect visages of his friends Katharine Hepburn, Elizabeth Taylor, and Sophia Loren—is close to Michael's heart. He seeks such beauty for himself.

Torn between his extraordinary empathy for the imperfectly figured and his obsession with the perfectly formed, Michael is both tolerant of differences in others and intolerant of flaws in himself. He never tires of studying the golden age of Hollywood photography of Horst P. Horst and George Hurrell, in which luminous stars like Greta Garbo and Gene Tierney are cast in alluring black-and-white, shadow-and-light shadings of unblemished beauty.

"Beauty's only skin-deep," sang the Temptations, a

Motown group that became one of the earliest models for Joseph Jackson's young sons. Michael knows the truth of that statement. Given his extreme sensitivity and empathetic nature, he seeks to pierce the veil of appearance and get to the heart of things. Yet veils and masks and cosmetic surgeries are as much a part of his life now as ever before.

He knows that in a few days he will be returning to the office of Dr. Klein, where Michael's appearance is the only concern. Now his concern is to quiet his mind, preoccupied, as always, with a million matters big and small: the managers, the shows, the dancers, the rehearsals, the stage, the special effects. If only he can quiet his mind, he can find sleep. But sleep, that most precious of commodities, eludes him.

11

Interlude

On the last Sunday in March, Michael is at the Wynn Las Vegas, where he has taken his children to see a show. While there, he has arranged to meet Dr. Conrad Murray on a matter of paramount importance: his peace of mind.

Michael realizes that this pernicious insomnia cannot go unattended. Murray agrees. They have a plan of action. But rather than reflect on the plan before he puts it into action, Michael prefers to listen to some of his own music. It comforts him to wax nostalgic about the last period in his life that could be called careless. These were his early years at Neverland; it was the first time he left his mother's home. This was before the accusations, the two marriages, the children, the continuous assaults from the press. Ironically, he titled the project that marks this period *Dangerous*, perhaps subconsciously aware of impending menace. At the time, the transition from *Off the Wall* to *Thriller* to *Bad* to *Dangerous* made sense. Michael is always motivated to raise the stakes.

During the course of the afternoon in his suite at the Wynn, he hears the title track, "Dangerous," and immediately feels a sense of pride. After three straight albums with Quincy Jones, part of the risk that Michael ran—indeed, part of the danger—was in deciding to self-produce. Having meticulously studied the techniques of the masters—Bobby Taylor, Berry Gordy, Hal Davis, Marvin Gaye, Stevie Wonder, Deke Richards, Kenny Gamble and Leon Huff, and Quincy—Michael felt ready by the beginning of the nineties to take the next step and break out on his own.

In the summer of 1990, when the production on *Dangerous* began, Michael turned thirty-two. The transition—going from the celebrated result of another producer's art to a full-fledged auteur—felt natural and necessary. But when it came to music, Michael has always walked the fine line between daring and caution. Daringly, he explores new sonic innovations and dives into new genres, as with the rock-centric "Beat It," from *Thriller*. But cautiously, he keeps his ear to the radio to discern what's trending in the fickle marketplace. Consequently, he looks at collaboration as a happy medium, employing the hottest hit makers to help him stay ahead of the curve.

His chief cohort in *Dangerous* is Teddy Riley, the enormously successful architect of new jack swing, the sound that reshaped rhythm and blues in the early nineties. Because rhythm and blues represents Michael's deepest roots, he feels most comfortable using that style as the basis for branching out with others.

"Michael wanted me to find new writers," said Dale

Kawashima, who ran Jackson's publishing company from 1987 through 1991, "but primarily those working in R & B. He wanted R & B hits and wanted to collaborate with R & B songwriters. He was raised in the Motown paradigm of crossing over from R & B to pop. For Michael, R & B was the starting point."

Now it's March 29, 2009, and it's time for Michael to start out for the office of Dr. Conrad Murray, time to institute their plan. His children remain behind with security in his hotel suite. Michael climbs into the black SUV and is driven through the glitzy desert city. He slips a CD of *Dangerous* into the audio player and leans back and listens to the explosive Teddy Riley dance tracks that open the record: "Jam," "Why You Wanna Trip on Me," "In the Closet," and "She Drives Me Wild." In the wake of other R & B hits — say, Bobby Brown's "My Prerogative" or "Every Little Step" — Michael is new jack swing on steroids. His is a bigger, noisier, more complex sonic construction. The album is unapologetically ambitious.

On the mid-tempo "Remember the Time," a look back on lost love, Michael, reflecting the percussive vocal influence of soul singer Billy Stewart, has never sung more passionately. The intensity never abates. "Black or White," his disquisition on racial bias, has the quality of a sing-along anthem. Equally anthemic in the rock arena is the blistering "Give In to Me," a song that Michael wrote with Bill Bottrell, another major collaborator on *Dangerous*. The vocal ferocity on this track and on "Who Is It," with its magnetic, "Billie Jean"–like movement, is almost frightening.

In stark contrast is "Will You Be There," which begins with a choral section of Beethoven's Ninth Symphony. Easily Michael's most remarkable opening, the hymn segues into a black church groove, with lush harmonies by gospel great Andraé Crouch, whose choir sustains a similar mood in "Keep the Faith." Perhaps the most poignant moment on *Dangerous* is when Michael transitions from the ferocious to the fragile in "Gone Too Soon," a touching eulogy for Ryan White, the courageous teenager felled by AIDS in 1990.

Michael considers the fallen. His heart aches for the abandoned and the sick, the neglected and the abused. Maybe, he thinks, that's one of the reasons he finds it so difficult to quiet his mind, whether during the day or at night. Quieting his mind is the purpose of this trip.

The SUV pulls up at Murray's office on East Flamingo Road, where the doctor is waiting. Michael remembers that Las Vegas is where Murray treated his children for the flu.

From Michael's standpoint, Murray is just a doctor willing to accede to his patient's wishes. Michael isn't aware of the enormous financial pressure plaguing Murray. Deeply in debt, the cardiologist is facing a number of lawsuits and judgments against him. Now, with the guarantee of being paid $150,000 a month to serve as Michael's personal physician, Murray is highly motivated to please the artist. His fiscal survival depends on keeping Michael happy and healthy.

When Michael and Murray arrive, Dr. David Adams, the anesthesiologist who sedated Michael and his son Blanket during dental procedures a year earlier, is waiting for them. It was Murray who, at Michael's urging, invited Adams to this meeting.

The three men go into Murray's office. There is an awkward silence. Adams has not been told the purpose of the encounter. Michael begins talking about the upcoming tour, explaining that he's only doing it so that his children might see him in the role of live entertainer. He doesn't want them to miss that experience.

Adams still isn't clear what his job would be.

After Murray leaves the room, Michael proceeds to interview Adams, asking him a series of personal questions. Satisfied with the answers, Michael speaks of his own plans to one day open a hospital for children.

Then, without explanation, Michael excuses himself and leaves Adams, who is still bewildered about why he has been called to the office. After conferring with Murray in another room, Michael returns. He tells Adams that during the upcoming tour he will need his rest. He wants the anesthesiologist to accompany him to London and stay there for the duration of the shows. From time to time, Michael explains, he may need an IV.

Murray joins them, and the three men segue into a discussion of finances. Adams is asked whether he'd consider suspending his practice to go on the road. Michael tells him that he doesn't need a decision today, but to please think about it. The meeting is over. Michael and the kids fly back to Los Angeles; he's hopeful that Adams will come on board. He's comforted by the thought that an additional physician—an anesthesiologist—will be there to treat his insomnia.

A few days later, Murray and Adams have a conversation. Adams wants to know the length of the commitment. Murray isn't certain. He says it's possible that there will be concerts beyond London, even a world tour. If he is to shut down his practice, Adams explains, he will need a guarantee of $100,000 a month for a minimum of three years.

The anesthesiologist never hears from Michael or Murray again.

12

April Fools' Day

Michael likes to play. Surprising everyone at the Carol-wood estate, he'll impetuously answer the ringing phone and disguise his voice, taking on the persona of some loony character. He'll engage the caller in a long conversation that sometimes concludes with Michael revealing his true identity and other times leaves the caller completely puzzled.

He loves water games. Ever since the sixties, when he and his brothers started dropping water balloons from hotel windows on unsuspecting pedestrians, he has kept up the routine in one form or another. He is famous for his prowess as a water gun fighter. "I'm the Michael Jordan of water guns," he once boasted.

When, for the first time ever, Michael celebrated Christmas—not recognized as a holiday by Jehovah's Witnesses—his first presents came from Elizabeth Taylor, who had taken it upon herself to lavishly decorate an enormous tree she had brought into his Neverland living room.

She gifted him with a set of Super Soakers, state-of-the-art water guns. Michael couldn't have been happier.

Many were the raucous times when, with Super Soaker in hand, Michael took on his sister Janet, his friends the young actors Emmanuel Lewis and Macaulay Culkin, his nephews and nieces, and whoever else might want to engage him in battle. He sees it all as high-spirited and harmless fun. To be soaked in water is to undergo a sort of secular baptism that bonds you with Michael and his sense of jocularity.

At the beginning of April of 2009, Michael calls his trainer, Lou Ferrigno, and, disguising his voice, identifies himself as "Omar." Omar has a long story to tell—about how much he has admired Ferrigno as an actor, how he has closely followed his career, how he considers Ferrigno one of the greatest men in the world today. Ferrigno is puzzled. He has no idea who Omar is and how he got his number. Omar goes on talking. Ferrigno tries to interrupt, but Omar can't be stopped. Only after ten minutes does Michael reveal himself. Ferrigno is amused and flattered that Michael Jackson has taken the time to joke with him.

Michael's pranks help him forget the weighty matters that await him once the jokes have played out. If he can maintain the mind of a child, he can avoid the decisions of an adult. And the more difficult those decisions, the greater the propensity for play. For decades, he has stolen away to Disneyland and other amusement parks the world over for weeks at a time, imagining such make-believe domains as permanent reality. From the day he bought the massive 2,700-acre property in the Santa Ynez Valley, in 1988, until the day he fled California for Bahrain, in 2005, Neverland was his own personal amusement park, an attempt to Disney-ize his day-to-day life in perpetuity.

"Michael's like a little kid who isn't happy till he has his playtime," said Frank Dileo. "When I met him in the eighties, that was the first thing I realized about that. And then when I caught up with him in 2009, I figured, because he had kids of his own, he'd be different. But I was wrong. He was more a kid than ever. The older he got, the younger he acted."

Back in 1995, six years after firing Dileo, Michael released *HIStory*, the most mythmaking of all his albums. Here he finally put to music the view he had adopted—and promulgated to the media—ever since he understood the importance of offering a thumbnail narrative of his life. He called the song, later used in the film *Free Willy 2: The Adventure Home*, "Childhood."

It is a plaintive ballad, with a schmaltzy but beautiful melody that could have easily been inserted into the score of *Oliver!* The refrain is the question, have we seen Michael's childhood? The presumed answer is no, because in Michael's mythology, he never had a childhood. In his autobiography and in many subsequent interviews, he bemoans the absence of a normal upbringing, which meant that he couldn't go out and play like other kids and feel free from the pressures of pleasing an audience, winning contests, securing gigs, and making money.

In the video for "Childhood," Michael sits alone in

what seems to be a lost forest, his isolation echoing the sentiment that he's looking for a past that he can neither recognize nor reclaim. He laments that he is forever misunderstood. And if he is guilty of "kidding around" like a child, that's because he's had to compensate for a childhood he never knew.

As he pleads to be not judged but, rather, loved, there is an ethereal image of young children on a revolving Disney-like ride of sail ships floating in a starlit sky. Michael sings of his "strange eccentricities" and his love of "elementary things," the oddities formed, in his understanding, by an absent childhood. At the end of the song, which is not without self-pity, his voice cracks and he appears close to tears as he reflects on what he calls his "painful youth."

In Michael's world, pain is often juxtaposed with play. Just as play is pain's antidote, pain is play's unspoken subtext. The more you hurt, the harder you play. They seem to be flip sides of the same coin, just as "Childhood" was the flip side of the first single from *HIStory*, "Scream," the space fantasy in which Michael and Janet play away their frustrations in an ingenious set of artistic games.

"Michael just doesn't simply think about childhood," said Bob Jones, the publicist who was a witness to both Michael's early and later years. "He reads about it. People think all he does is watch cartoons, but Michael's a serious reader. He reads Shakespeare, especially the tragedies and history plays, not just for the stories but for the psychology of the characters. He reads all sorts of psychology. It was

Michael who also turned me on to Jean-Jacques Rousseau, the French philosopher who wrote about childhood and the way to raise kids."

The work by Rousseau that undoubtedly appealed to Michael is *Emile, or On Education*. Published in 1762, the book argues that children must be understood before they are taught; that they must be given the freedom to be children, not molded into precursors of themselves as adults; that they must learn morality through the natural consequences of their actions, not through corporal punishment. In short, Rousseau's prescription for the ideal childhood was the exact opposite of Michael's experience.

So on April Fools' Day in 2009, Michael is delighted to play all sorts of innocent tricks on and childish games with his children. He revels in the emotional freedom he has afforded them. He is committed to making sure that they can, as Rousseau suggested, enjoy the beauty of childhood for its own sake.

The month starts off on an especially positive note, with the hiring of Kai Chase, a chef who has been interviewed and approved by Michael's children. She observes what seems to her a happy household: a vigorous father who is attentive to his children and rarely misses a meal with them; children who respond beautifully to their homeschooling; a family interested in a healthy lifestyle; and, in Grace Rwaramba, the children's nanny, a woman who lovingly plays the role of surrogate mother.

Michael's mother would not approve, but on Friday,

April 3, 2009, her son again refuses to reconcile himself with the religious practices of his past—practices that he once held sacrosanct. April 3 is Paris's eleventh birthday, and in defiance of the Jehovah's Witness directive that birthdays *not* be celebrated, Michael *will* celebrate this day and shower his daughter with loving affection and presents galore. There's an enormous Lilo and Stitch birthday cake, plus circus performers in the backyard. For this one day, healthy foods give way to pizza, hot wings, and banana splits. Paris has chosen to decorate the dining room with a birthday theme: Michael Jackson. Concert posters are taped to the walls, and Michael's music plays nonstop.

Later that day, Michael and the kids, with security in tow, head out in the blue Escalades to downtown Beverly Hills. Like most everyone in consumer-crazed America, he is vulnerable to the seductive delights of shopping. His history as an impulsive and intemperate spender is well documented. He buys impetuously and extravagantly. Big buying is another way to beat back the blues. Purchasing on a grand scale produces its own kind of high. Michael thinks back on the major purchases of his life—an extensive variety of exotic animals, the Beatles song catalog, Neverland—and remembers the joys that come with ownership.

He wants his beloved daughter to experience such joy. As they enter the Rolex store on Rodeo Drive, Paris is wearing a veil, a covering to protect her identity but also to signal her uniqueness. Like all three Jackson children,

Paris has been made to feel special. Michael indulges his children, as any wealthy father would, but he also imposes restraints. They can only have so much. The last thing he wants to do is spoil them, yet he is conscious that he spoils himself. But is it spoiling himself or merely allowing himself pleasures denied during his youth?

Given a lifetime of relentless work, he reasons, doesn't he deserve the comfort of surrounding himself and his loved ones with beautiful things? If he has amassed an enormous collection of art, much of it in the category of extreme kitsch, it's because of the delight he takes in acquiring and displaying works that excite his spirit. Isn't he entitled?

"People forget that we're a working-class family who had to struggle and struggle hard for everything we've achieved," said Janet Jackson. "For years, Michael denied himself the simple things people take for granted, like holidays and vacations. So when he achieved success, how could he not feel entitled to indulge himself in buying beautiful things? Who could blame him?"

"Just like a junkie gets hooked on smack, I've known a slew of entertainers hooked on spending," said Ray Charles, who lived a frugal life. "'Cause they're out there on the road, sweating and straining, they think they've earned the right to buy up everything in sight — houses, cars, jewelry, all kinds of junk they don't even need. They do it to fill a hole in their soul. I can understand it, 'cause it's lonely out there. Feels good to be in the spotlight. Feels good to hear all that applause. But when they turn off the spotlight and the clapping stops, you start hungering for something else to make you feel good."

Indulging Paris on her birthday undoubtedly makes Michael feel good. Going on buying binges has always had a salutary effect. In Michael's mind, making major purchases is an act that affirms his faith in his future. It reassures him that everything will be all right.

The fierce discipline that he has used to hone his skills as a singer, dancer, and writer has never been applied to his finances. When the money started streaming in in the sixties and seventies, his father was in control. In the eighties, when Michael tried managing himself, there was so much money that the idea of fiscal limits seemed ludicrous. New managers—Ron Weisner, Freddy DeMann, Frank Dileo—ultimately became ex-managers when Michael resisted the idea of managerial restraint. Now, in the spring of 2009, as he continues to pit one manager against another, he falls back into the familiar pattern of acting as though his money will never run out.

And why should he think otherwise? He will always be able to write and record new songs. He will always be able to perform. He will always be able to entertain people the world over. He will always be able to earn their love and respect. In turn, they will always be willing to pay him handsomely for his artistic services. Their loyalty will never waver.

To Michael, these are plain facts. He can earn as much as he wants. He can buy as much as he wants.

He can't restrain himself. He doesn't try.

But at night, when he does try to sleep, the same battle ensues.

Why can't he clear his mind?

Why can't he, like his precious children, simply drift off and enjoy the simple satisfaction of deep and undisturbed sleep?

13

Milk

Some physicians call it the milk of amnesia. Michael simply calls it milk. In Michael's mind, the resemblance of propofol, the powerful sleep-inducing agent, to the dairy product casts the drug in a friendlier light. Milk is good for you. Michael feels the same about propofol. Over the past decades he has tried countless sleep-inducing medicines, with increasingly frustrating results. None of them are able to shut down the machinery of his overactive mind. None of them can stop the all-night ruminations, the endless loop of entangled thoughts that torture him to the point of desperation. The relentless mental pain of chronic insomnia is enough to drive a sane man mad. Michael is convinced that no one understands the depths of his suffering. No one understands his body chemistry the way he does. As a studious observer of all things, he has closely monitored the impact of various medicines on his bodily behavior, and he believes he knows exactly what he needs to sleep.

The problem is that propofol is an intravenous anesthetic whose use is restricted to operating rooms, where its dispensation can be properly supervised and monitored by an anesthesiologist. But because over a long period of time Michael has convinced various professionals — dentists, plastic surgeons, and dermatologists — to inject him with propofol during painful treatments, he is certain that the drug is safe.

On April 6, 2009, Dr. Conrad Murray, at his client's request, orders the first shipment of propofol from a pharmaceutical firm in Las Vegas. Murray, who still hasn't been formally hired by AEG, won't actually stay at the Carolwood estate until May. On this evening in April, though, Cherilyn Lee, a registered nurse who has already made several visits to Michael's home in 2009, arrives to advise him about nutrition, her specialty. In the past she has served him protein drinks designed to boost his energy.

In earlier meetings with Lee, Michael mentioned the benefits of propofol in promoting his sleep. Unfamiliar with the drug, Lee looked it up in the *Physicians' Desk Reference* and was alarmed at what she found. She now reads the entry to Michael, pointing out the dangers and the critical fact that it should be administered only in a hospital setting.

Michael has heard all this before. He remains unconvinced and continues arguing his point: that many of his physicians have freely given him propofol. They have assured him of its safety. He has taken it in the past and it has worked wonders. With strenuous rehearsals on the horizon, he needs at least eight hours of sleep. He assures

Lee that he doesn't like drugs. He never uses them for recreational purposes, never gets high. He takes medicine only when necessary, and he takes only what physicians have pronounced 100 percent safe. Propofol is safe, he says. And when it comes to guaranteeing sleep, nothing but propofol will do the job.

For all his cajoling, Lee stands firm. Even when she tells Michael that taking propofol could mean that he might never wake up, he remains adamant, arguing that as long as she is there to monitor him, there is no danger.

Ignoring Michael's request, the nurse gives him an herbal remedy and tucks him into bed as a mother would a child. Like a child, Michael is watching a Donald Duck cartoon on his computer. When Lee suggests that he shut down the device, he resists, explaining that cartoons are part of his ritual. In addition, soft classical music is piped in over loudspeakers. The combination of Disney characters and orchestral melodies calms Michael to the point that he can finally fall asleep.

Four hours later, though, he awakens, visibly rattled. He tells Lee, who has been sitting in a chair in the corner of his bedroom, that this is what always happens. He says that even if he does manage to sleep, it's never for more than three or four hours. He can't tolerate such a situation. Only propofol can help. Only propofol gets him the rest he needs.

Seeing that the nurse will not submit to his request, he thanks her nonetheless. He gives her a farewell hug and expresses gratitude for her concern. Michael sees Cherilyn Lee as a loving and nurturing caretaker. But because she doesn't buy into the notion that, when it comes to medicine, Michael knows just what is needed, he will never summon her to the house again.

♪ ♪ ♪

Michael is seductive. His singing, his dancing, his stage persona, his offstage personality, his whole aura of natural charm, draw you to him. He has wielded the power of his celebrity with calculated skill. Over and over again, he has described himself as shy. Perhaps. But if so, he has slyly used his shyness and whisper-quiet voice to achieve his own ends. This has been especially true in his relationships with physicians, many of whom he has subtly seduced into giving him what he wants.

The case of Arnold Klein, who in the spring of 2009 continues to treat Michael with Botox and inject him with Demerol, is especially telling. Long ago, Klein was drawn into Michael's inner circle. That meant VIP access to Michael's concerts and invitations to Michael's home. It meant becoming Michael's close personal friend. But was it as a friend or a physician that Klein provided Michael with the facial treatments designed to preserve his youth and the medicines to dull the pain? For Michael, there was no boundary between the professional and the personal. That's why he so nimbly denies his dependence on drugs. How could you call it an addiction? Well-respected physicians, Michael reasons, are prescribing these medicines.

Would they do so if they felt that he had an addiction problem? Beyond that, these physicians are his personal friends. They not only care for him; they love him. Would loving friends dispense medicines that would in any way harm him? Of course not.

So to those, like sister Janet, who question his relationship to drugs and even attempt to intervene, Michael responds irately. He does not require rehab. He is fine. His drug intake is under control. He is, in fact, under the supervision of experienced doctors like Arnold Klein and Conrad Murray, men who, in Michael's mind, have made their mark on the medical community and always have his best interests at heart.

In mid-April, rehearsals begin at CenterStaging, in Burbank. Michael only occasionally drops in to check on the progress. Instead, he works at home with his choreographer, Travis Payne, on a regular basis. He also continues to vacillate between warring managers. He is not at all certain which ones truly care about him. After the initial meeting at Carolwood with his father and Leonard Rowe, he cut off contact with them. But they, as well as Michael's mother, have persisted. They have insisted that they see him again. The letter naming Rowe as Michael's manager remains unsigned, as does the resolution for plans for a Jacksons reunion concert underwritten by promoter Patrick Allocco.

Given Michael's contractual obligation to do fifty shows

in London, advisors are urging him to avoid another meeting with those determined to undermine his relationship with AEG. The result would be a legal nightmare. But Michael, wanting to please Mother, agrees to the meeting with Joseph, Leonard Rowe, and Patrick Allocco, this one at Sportsmen's Lodge, in Studio City, where he signs the letter — anything to placate this group. In a handwritten addendum, though, Michael states that Rowe is being appointed for "financial overseeing only" and that this decision "can be revoked at any time."

The letter is written to Randy Phillips at AEG, who is more uncertain than ever about who is managing Michael and what this means for the immediate future.

Frank Dileo, Michael's "Uncle Tookie" and the manager for whom he holds the warmest sentiment, has been working both sides of the street. He initially forged an agreement with Rowe to facilitate the reunion concert. But now he is edging his way into the AEG camp. In the wake of so much confusion, Dileo does not have a hard time persuading Phillips that, given his long and successful history with Michael, he and he alone can win back the artist's trust.

But who *can* Michael trust?

For now, trust is not the issue. He simply wants to make himself happy by making everyone else happy. He wants peace with his father, peace with his mother, peace with his siblings, peace with his old managers and new managers, peace with his old promoters and new promoters.

Yes, he'll agree to do whatever the world wants.

Yes, he'll not only please his fans; he'll thrill them. He'll give them all he's got—and then some.

He'll sign this piece of paper. He'll sign that piece of paper.

He'll bring all these forces together as only he can.

He'll do all this in the name of love.

And in doing it, he prays, he'll find the ultimate peace: the peace of mind that will allow him to close his eyes and sleep.

14

Disappear into
the Dance

In April of 2009, Michael watches 1951's *Royal Wedding*. As Fred Astaire, in top hat and tails, returns to his hotel room, he reflects on his infatuation with a beautiful young woman. Astaire breaks into a song—"You're All the World to Me"—but singing alone can't express the joy in his heart: he's gotta dance. And dance he does, up the side of one wall and then down the side of another. But even that feat can't contain his romantic energy. His gravity-defying artistry has him dancing on the ceiling, leaping and spinning with the kind of lyrical dexterity that Michael has been emulating ever since he was first exposed to Fred Astaire–Ginger Rogers movies when he was a teenager.

"He'd play Fred and I'd play Ginger," said sister Janet. "We'd be doing the dances as we watched the movies— *Top Hat, The Barkleys of Broadway, Follow the Fleet, Shall We Dance.* Michael was the perfect Astaire. He had that ease of movement, that smoothness that made dancing as natural as walking. He'd patiently teach me the intricate steps until we had perfected the routines. During other times in my childhood Michael could be less than kind, but not when it came to dancing. He was the sweetest teacher you can imagine. He had us both floating on air. He used to say that he wanted to do what Astaire did— disappear into the dance."

Michael adores Astaire. So great is his respect for the dancer that he dedicated his autobiography to the man. Years ago, Michael had to obtain copies of Astaire movies in order to watch them, but now there is YouTube, where every enchanting Astaire routine is accessible in a second. Renewing his love of the dancer's relaxed-beyond-reason demeanor, Michael watches Astaire as Rod Riley, the dancing detective in *The Band Wagon*, directed by Vincente Minnelli, father of Michael's friend Liza. This is the character that Michael reimagined in his "Smooth Criminal" video from 1988. Michael not only wears a replica of Astaire's white suit/blue shirt/white tie/white fedora outfit, he mimics the moves of the master, the gentle tough guy whose dancing feet will defeat a gang of notorious hoodlums. He goes so far as to literally quote Astaire's description of statuesque costar Cyd Charisse when, at the beginning of "Dangerous," Michael muses, "She came at me in sections . . . The girl was dangerous . . . The girl was bad."

For Michael, dancing must reflect an edge of danger, that same sort of street danger that, as a child, he recognized in the moves of James Brown. Astaire's cinematic version of danger, in which a threatening situation is squeezed into a set piece — a compact narrative that unfolds in five or six minutes — became the template for Michael's string of extravagant videos in the eighties, starting with "Billie Jean." When Michael managed to combine Brown's dark funk with Astaire's airy elegance, he created a style whose appeal cut across all class and racial divides.

But Michael goes much further than either James Brown or Fred Astaire. If dance is danger, he pushes that danger to the limit. As Michael's song from 1997 says, there's "blood on the dance floor." Dance, his lyrics explain, is his escape. That escape is sometimes violent. In the extended version of the "Black or White" video, for example, a black panther wanders through the set and into a back lot. The panther then morphs into Michael, who breaks into an astounding dance that's void of music. For nearly five minutes, Michael has what amounts to a syncopated nervous breakdown. Incensed by the swastika and racist epithets — "Nigger go home," "No more wetbacks" — scribbled on the windows of an abandoned vehicle, he dances the car into destruction, smashing its windows with a tire iron. Rather than sing, he screams his frustrations, like a werewolf howling at the moon. He sexualizes his rage by stroking his crotch and ripping at his shirt before remorphing into the animal from which he emerged. Then, as if to signal that it's all a harmless fantasy, the music returns, the "Black or White" groove is reestablished, and we see Bart Simpson watching Michael's video before Homer grabs the remote and, complaining about the loud noise, flicks off the TV.

For Michael, the dance ritual runs the gamut from the innocence of Shirley Temple, his favorite child star, to the deadly violence of *West Side Story*, his favorite musical. Often — as in "Black or White" — he is able to combine these elements: the sublime and the sinister, the carefree and the callous, the cheery and the menacing. Like his singing range, his dancing range is remarkable — another outlet for turning his unfiltered feelings into art.

Michael spends a mid-April morning watching YouTube clips of his short films — the term he prefers to "videos" — to remind himself of the routines he must re-master for his comeback concerts. Over the years, his choreography has become increasingly complex and demanding. There is the graveyard frivolity of "Thriller"; the gang warring in "Beat It" (echoing *West Side Story*); the Martin Scorsese–directed subway drama "Bad"; the hyper-heterosexualized "The Way You Make Me Feel"; the celebrity-studded "Liberian Girl"; the gangster-leaning "Smooth Criminal," with its startling call-and-response interlude; the self-mocking "Leave Me Alone"; the glittery, Egyptian-edged "Remember the Time"; the ambitious "Heal the World"; the daring "Give In to Me"; the spacey "Scream"; the brooding "Stranger in Moscow"; the Spike Lee–directed, Brazil-set "They Don't Care About Us"; the epic "Ghosts"; and the barroom-brawling "You Rock My World" (with cameos from Chris Tucker and Marlon Brando).

Michael revels in the originality of the choreography.

But mimicking these short films in live concerts requires more than originality; it requires verisimilitude. Michael must craft dance routines and employ dancers who give the audience the impression of the original videos that have been viewed millions of times. This is a formidable chore.

As he is driven from the Carolwood estate to the Kodak Theatre, Michael considers the backbreaking work of putting together a show. Until now, he has left it to others to scrutinize the hundreds of prospective dancers who have assembled in Los Angeles. Psychologically, he was not ready to face the work. But today is different. Today he has decided that he can no longer ignore the calls imploring him to get more hands-on with the staging of the show. Today is the final audition for dancers. Today Michael is showing up.

As he looks out the window and reflects on the smoggy Hollywood afternoon, he is not happy that some of his original ideas have been scrapped. With P. T. Barnum in mind, Michael envisioned a glorious stage entrance at London's O_2 that no one would ever forget. He proposed that he ride in on the back of a bejeweled elephant. Sitting next to him would be three monkeys. Panthers, on gold chains, would stride beside him. Flocks of parrots and rare exotic birds would fly overhead. His fans would go wild. But when PETA (People for the Ethical Treatment of Animals) and the Captive Animals' Protection Society got wind of the plans, they protested. They sternly admonished Michael that the era of tolerating animal exploitation of this variety was long over. Realizing that he was, in fact, out of step with the times, Michael scrapped his proposal.

He arrives at the Kodak Theatre wondering whether some of his other ideas are also anomalies. It has been thirteen long years since *HIStory*, the last time he mounted a major show. Since then, the world of entertainment has radically changed. He worries that he is not altogether current. Might this show run the risk of appearing old-fashioned or out-of-date? The idea is intolerable. It can't happen. It won't happen. Michael won't let it happen.

He is reassured when, seated next to his director, Kenny Ortega, he watches the final group of dancers vying for spots in his show. The dancers are superb. He moves closer to the stage to get a better look. Michael judges their suitability for his show not merely by their moves but by the look in their eyes. Do they have that fire? That desire? Are they able to lose themselves in the routine? Can they disappear into the dance?

Michael is satisfied that they can. In his judgment, the group he chooses is among the best he has ever employed. For some of the set pieces, he will do what he has always done: re-create the feeling of the Jackson 5 by sharing the stage with four male dancers. This is the lineup he has known since he started out in the sixties, a lineup that affords him a sense of comfort and reassurance. On songs like "Smooth Criminal" and "They Don't Care About Us," he will double the number of male dancers to eight. A sensuous female dancer will provoke his moves in "The Way You Make Me Feel."

The dancers are in place. Kenny Ortega, a man Michael trusts, is steering the mighty ship with a steady hand. Michael has dozens of ideas about innovations and improvements for the show, but now, he decides, is not the time to delineate them. To do so would be too exhausting. He must protect his energy. He must allow Ortega to direct. It's more than two months before the London opening. Right now he wants these rehearsals to take their course without him. He leaves the theater feeling that, although the demands upon him to whip the show into tip-top shape are tremendous, those demands can wait.

Like the enormity of his show, the enormity of his managerial problem is something he'd rather not consider. He'll get to it later. One day at a time, one decision at a time.

On April 17, he pays still another visit to the Beverly Hills office of Dr. Arnold Klein. Having expressed concern about perspiring during his performances, Michael was told that Botox applied to the axillae — the underarms — will help. The application is painful. Thus Michael is given three hundred milligrams of Demerol, the drug that he finds so alluring.

That evening, becalmed by his medical treatment, he turns to one of his other soothing balms: shopping. With ever-present security in tow, he's off to Book Soup on Sunset Boulevard, a well-stocked store favored by serious readers. He thinks first of his kids. He picks out a pile of children's books before moving over to the music section, where he peruses tomes on himself. He's amazed at how many there are. Presuming that they are filled with misinformation, he cares less about the content than he does about his images on the covers. He carefully considers the way the books physically portray him. He feels that they feature less than flattering photographs. Why do they inevitably choose pictures in which he looks disheveled or, even worse, grotesque? Why do they portray him as some sort of monster? Michael lumps his biographers in the same category as the paparazzi: insatiable vultures looking to pick him apart.

He sees that there are several copies of his own book, *Moonwalk*, on the shelves, although he wrote it back in the eighties. He remembers the agony that accompanied its publication. He had agreed to write it with the help of a ghostwriter at the behest of Jacqueline Kennedy Onassis, then an editor at Doubleday. He considered the former First Lady a great woman and was deeply flattered when she approached him. But then came the anguish of shaping his story. Before this, he had never stopped to consider what it meant to narrate the critical events of his life. He struggled with the process and procrastinated for years.

"While he loved books and carried them with him wherever he went, creating one was just not as exciting as finding the right note or step or guitarist," explained his editor, Shaye Areheart. "So the writing of this book took a long time."

When he did agree to be interviewed, Michael dwelled

on his childhood and the cruelty of his father. After Michael himself, his father, Joseph, emerges as *Moonwalk's* most memorable character.

Michael rejected the work of the first ghostwriter and began consulting directly with Areheart. Eventually a second writer, Stephen Davis, was employed, although his name did not appear on the book's cover. After finally approving the contents and allowing the book to go to press, Michael had a crisis of conscience. He worried that the memoir would alienate his family. He was especially concerned about his descriptions of the beatings he suffered at Joseph's hand. He feared that he had been too candid. Through Michael's attorney, John Branca, Doubleday was instructed to scrub the project. At the last minute, though, the publisher persuaded Michael to release the book, which immediately became a bestseller.

Michael loves books and bookstores. In addition to Book Soup, he has been a regular customer at the area's biggest independent stores: Dutton's, in Brentwood; Skylight, in Los Feliz; and Hennessey + Ingalls, specialists in books on architecture and art, in Santa Monica. One of his favorite features of the Carolwood estate is the wood-paneled library. His holdings in Neverland include ten thousand books.

An autodidact, Michael has always been attracted to self-help tomes. He was intimately familiar with the essential self-affirmation books, from Norman Vincent Peale's

The Power of Positive Thinking to Og Mandino's *The Greatest Salesman in the World.* He read Joseph Murphy's *The Power of Your Subconscious Mind* and Shakti Gawain's *Creative Visualization.* From Berry Gordy he learned to love the nineteenth-century poem "If" by Rudyard Kipling, which concludes with lines that Michael took to heart:

If you can fill the unforgiving minute
With sixty seconds' worth of distance run,
Yours is the Earth and everything that's in it,
And — which is more — you'll be a man, my son!

Michael's favorite philosopher-poet, Ralph Waldo Emerson, also wrote in the nineteenth century. Several times Michael read Emerson's famous essay on self-reliance. Emerson's contemporary Herman Melville spoke to Michael through his epic, *Moby-Dick.* Michael related to the novelist's obsession with the ultimate catch. Michael never tires of reading to his children the books and stories that he loved as a child: "Rip Van Winkle," *Treasure Island,* and of course *Peter Pan.*

Michael's hunger for information is insatiable. Learned teachers who befriended him, like Rabbi Shmuley Boteach, have noted the wide range of his intellectual curiosity.

"Even when Michael doesn't have time to read the books, he loves the feeling of being surrounded by them," said Bob Jones, who helped curate the Neverland library. "He once told me that books exude a spirit that, even [when] unread, he can feel. He knows that knowledge is a precious commodity. No matter the circumstance, he never stops seeking knowledge. He also knows that knowledge is power, and I think it's fair to say that Michael is a man interested in amassing the kind of power that edifies."

His purchases at Book Soup brighten Michael's mood. He looks forward to considering new ideas, exploring new stories, listening to the reassuring voices of writers with the wisdom to tame the storm that all too often assaults his soul.

Reading long into the night is another way to induce sleep. Michael can take his mind off himself and the pressing problems. He can read himself into oblivion.

At some point, though, the excitement of the book wears off. His eyes are heavy with slumber and he can no longer focus on the words on the printed page. The words blur. The ideas scatter. His body is bone-tired. But his mind is awake.

15

Heat

Monday, April 20, 2009, is a scorcher. It's over a hundred degrees in downtown L.A., the hottest day of the year.

The heat is on Michael to meet about the design of the show.

The heat is on Michael to show up for rehearsals.

The heat is on Michael to finally make a decision about a manager.

But Michael ignores the heat. Michael is cool. Michael is moving, as he always does, to the beat of his own drummer. He's playing with the kids, trying to calm them down. They're upset because their nanny, Grace Rwaramba, has been fired. No reason is given. It may well be that Michael fears that the children's attachment to Grace has become greater than their attachment to him. Michael reassures his kids that, more than ever, he will be with them night and day. He is the only parent they need.

To keep things on the upbeat, he watches YouTube clips of the tap-dancing Nicholas Brothers. Their acrobatic routine from the film *Stormy Weather*, which floored him as a child, floors him again. He flashes back to when, in the seventies, he and his brothers danced with the Nicholases on national television — a highlight of the Jackson 5 days. *Stormy Weather* has Michael thinking of Lena Horne, whom he met when she played Glinda the Good Witch in *The Wiz*. He watches the exquisite twenty-five-year-old Lena sing the title song in *Stormy Weather* before watching the equally exquisite sixty-one-year-old Lena sing "Believe in Yourself," the emotional climax of *The Wiz*. As much as Michael adored Diana Ross and loved working with her on *The Wiz*, it was Lena Horne, he told friends, who stole the show and brought tears to his eyes when she appeared, in all her glory, as an angel of determination and hope.

Determination and hope are on Michael's mind as he ignores the mounting messages from the outside world.

Determination and hope, he knows, are what will get him through this long crisis of the soul that has clung to him ever since he announced the This Is It shows.

Michael has felt himself growing increasingly anxious, experiencing what he fears might be panic attacks. With that in mind, he visited Dr. Allan Metzger, who prescribed a couple of medicines: clonazepam, to treat the anxiety, and trazodone, an antidepressant commonly used to promote sleep.

The anxiety has been somewhat assuaged, but not the dreaded sleeplessness. While many claim good results using trazodone, Michael has no such luck. Time and again, he experiences medicine that should be soporific as stimulating. He's fed up with experimenting with drugs that he knows full well are not going to work. He knows what works: propofol for sleep and Demerol for pain.

There is a degree of pain — or at least discomfort — on Tuesday, April 21, when he returns from the Beverly Hills office of Arnold Klein, described by some as Michael's go-to Dr. Feelgood. The cause of the discomfort is the application of large quantities of Botox, followed by three hundred milligrams of Demerol. When the treatments are over, Michael silently slips out of the office, donning a hoodie and a surgical mask.

But by midweek Michael can no longer use the distractions of Botox treatments and shopping sprees to avoid making a managerial decision. Three different men have represented themselves as Michael's guy. The uncertainty is especially distressing to AEG, whose multimillion-dollar investment in Michael mushrooms with every passing day. The company needs to know the name of Michael's appointed representative. Who has his trust? Who can honestly say that he is speaking for him?

If AEG's Randy Phillips could easily get Michael on the phone, things would be different. But Michael is purposefully inaccessible. He has been this way for decades. Let others guess his intentions. Let others discern his motives. Michael likes camouflage. He revels in mystery. It pleases him that those underwriting his art — particularly promoters and record executives — do not know what he's thinking or planning.

But, while that strategy may have worked when Michael

was on top, working the comeback trail is a different deal. Being kept afloat by AEG, he can no longer sidestep the issue of representation.

The candidates are:

Current manager Tohme Tohme, brother Jermaine's friend, the man who brought in AEG and defines himself as the chief architect of Michael's financial resurrection.

Leonard Rowe, his father's friend, who claims there's an easier way to make a fortune than fifty grueling shows. Rowe argues that one colossal reunion concert will rake in millions.

Frank Dileo, the former Epic promo man from the *Thriller* and *Bad* glory days, who reminds Michael that, under his guidance, those glory days can return.

Dileo convinces Michael to sign a letter—written by Dileo in Michael's voice—to AEG, saying that Tohme Tohme will not serve as "production manager" during the This Is It shows.

Three days later, AEG informs Tohme Tohme that he is out.

Dileo is in.

It appears that some of the old guard, including attorney John Branca, may well be making a comeback of their own.

For Michael, it's back to the future.

Michael makes decisions with gnawing equivocation. He liked Tohme Tohme. He thought the man had good ideas. He leaned on him heavily for the better part of a year. Tohme Tohme represented a break from the past and fresh hope for the future. But if what Dileo says is true, Tohme Tohme has been exaggerating his connection to the world's most powerful media moguls. He doesn't have access to the billions of dollars required to make the kind of movies Michael has dreamed of producing and starring in.

Yet while Tohme Tohme was on the scene, Michael relied on his judgment. He felt that the man sincerely cared. As with every close advisor to Michael, it was more than a professional relationship. Tohme Tohme gave Michael the feeling that it was a personal relationship based on genuine love.

In fact, everyone around Michael can't help loving him. Michael elicits sympathy. His vulnerability attracts caretakers. The problem is that the desire to help him — even save him — is more often than not corrupted by greed. To get close to Michael is to get close to his money. To care for Michael is to care for his money.

The question for Michael has always been one of the quality of care — no easy task. The moneymen surrounding him have, for the most part, always been charming, successful, energetic, and brimming with confidence. Michael has wanted to believe in the sincerity of their efforts.

Yet when things go wrong — when, for example, *Bad,* for all its success, fails to sell anywhere near his unrealistic goal of one hundred million copies — Michael tends to turn on those advisors who have reinforced his fantasy projections. Drawn to men whose grandiose vision matches his own, he quickly loses faith in those same men when the vision isn't realized.

At the same time, Michael, more emotionally fragile than ever, lacks the psychic energy to build still another new managerial relationship. He recoils at the idea of going through that arduous process. The path of least resistance leads him back to familiar faces, old friends he once abandoned. Now in crisis mode—*Can I shake my lethargy and find the drive to whip the This Is It show into shape? Can I put my trust in the ever-controlling AEG?*—Michael feels the need for old friends. It's easy to forget the reasons they were once fired. Those were old suspicions, old fears. This is a new day.

In the struggle between darkness and light, Michael tries gallantly to move toward the light, no matter how faint the glow.

On the same day that he fires Tohme Tohme, Michael is still in search of a glowing facial image. He returns to Klein's office, where he is treated with not only Botox but Restylane, a filler used to smooth out the skin and eliminate wrinkles and crow's-feet. The medicine is injected into Michael's lips and right cheek. It's an uncomfortable procedure followed by an even larger dose of Demerol than usual—375 milligrams. Because the condition of his skin has become increasingly problematic, he's given a prescription for Ultravate to relieve irritation. When he leaves the office, Michael is wearing a black fedora. His eyes are hidden behind dark aviator glasses, his face is wrapped in a black cloth, and his mouth is covered by a blue surgical mask. He looks like a mummy.

To distract himself from his physical discomfort, he decides to go shopping, this time for antiques.

Chandeliers so fabulous that they look as though they could have hung in the Palace of Versailles; majestic stone lions to grace the entrance of Prince Jefri's Las Vegas estate, which Michael still fervently hopes to buy; massive oil paintings of pastoral scenes and proud aristocrats from an earlier era; gilded Queen Anne armchairs covered in scarlet silk; Victorian armoires of carved walnut; statuaries of kissing cherubs and weeping angels; hand-painted porcelain plates; jade pottery from ancient China; medieval tapestries; trinkets from India—enough stuff to furnish a mansion. Some of it is authentic, some of it fake. Michael doesn't differentiate, doesn't care: if the object is truly beautiful, if it sings to his soul and lifts his heart, that's enough. Shop owners are only too happy to extend to him all the credit he needs. To buy without restraint affirms Michael's commitment to a future filled with unlimited possibilities: more lovely things, more lovely days, more time at home with his children, more peace, more calm, more life lived without anguish or fear.

By the weekend, the fear and anguish are back. The side effects from the Botox and Restylane have left him in excruciating pain. On Saturday, April 25, Arnold Klein opens his office just to attend to Michael, this time giving him a full battery of treatments, including intralesional steroid therapy. Michael remains there for nearly five hours, not leaving until 9:30 p.m., with a prescription for prednisone.

On Monday morning, Michael is back at Klein's, this time in the company of his kids. Another three hundred milligrams of Demerol, more Restylane, more Botox. Afterward, more shopping. He and the children stop at the Ed Hardy store. In spite of being hounded by hysterical fans and aggressive paparazzi, Michael manages to do his shopping, leaving with twenty bags of merchandise.

On Tuesday and Thursday, April 28 and 30, Michael makes two more treks to Klein's office. Meanwhile, Dr. Conrad Murray, still waiting for an employment contract from AEG, is nonetheless ordering a variety of strong sleep-inducing medicines for Michael—among them lorazepam and midazolam—as well as a second supply of propofol.

Murray knows that keeping his patient healthy is more than a matter of sanctioning Michael's intermittent sessions with muscleman Lou Ferrigno. Michael must start getting a good night's sleep.

To Michael, it seems that sleep should be the easiest, the most natural thing in the world. We breathe, we eat, we drink, we sleep.

At night, wary of so many ineffective drugs, Michael tries drifting off by reading Shakespeare.

"Shakespeare was Michael's go-to poet," said Bob Jones, his personal publicist for over three decades. "He never tired of reading the Bard."

Now Michael is seeking out those passages concerning his nightly vexation. The most famous and relatable is from *Henry IV, Part 2.* The king is afflicted with the same maddening malady as Michael: chronic insomnia. Henry envies those citizens — the lowly, the poor — who can achieve what he, a mighty ruler, cannot. He laments how even a cabin boy in the midst of a raging storm is able to sleep. Playing the part of the king, Michael mouths the monarch's words:

How many thousand of my poorest subjects
Are at this hour asleep! O sleep, O gentle sleep,
Nature's soft nurse, how have I frighted thee,
That thou no more wilt weigh my eyelids down
And steep my senses in forgetfulness?
Why rather, sleep, liest thou in smoky cribs,
Upon uneasy pallets stretching thee
And hush'd with buzzing night-flies to thy slumber,
Than in the perfumed chambers of the great,
Under the canopies of costly state,
And lull'd with sound of sweetest melody?
O thou dull god, why liest thou with the vile
In loathsome beds, and leavest the kingly couch
A watch-case or a common 'larum-bell?
Wilt thou upon the high and giddy mast
Seal up the ship-boy's eyes, and rock his brains
In cradle of the rude imperious surge
And in the visitation of the winds,
Who take the ruffian billows by the top,

Curling their monstrous heads and hanging them
With deafening clamor in the slippery clouds,
That, with the hurly, death itself awakes?
Canst thou, O partial sleep, give thy repose
To the wet sea-boy in an hour so rude,
And in the calmest and most stillest night,
With all appliances and means to boot,
Deny it to a king? Then happy low, lie down!
Uneasy lies the head that wears a crown.

As the King of Pop, Michael's crown is just as heavy, his unease just as vexing. He relates to the line that says sleep is "nature's soft nurse."

He yearns for that nurse.

16

Wordless

Michael loves the high Elizabethan language of Shakespeare. He has seen the plays and films about Hamlet and Lear and Macbeth. He appreciates these characters' complexity. But sometimes language, especially the loftiest, taxes his mind. Sometimes he wishes to avoid even simple song lyrics. Sometimes he wants to lose himself in wordless music.

At the start of May of 2009, Kai Chase, the chef who had been told she would accompany the family to London, is dismissed by Michael's assistant, Michael Amir. No reason is given. Michael is preoccupied with the upcoming shows. He knows he has less than ten short weeks to prepare for the London opening. He knows he needs to be more conscientious. Having missed many rehearsals and meetings, he also knows that without his hands-on participation, the shows will suffer. At the same time, he knows himself. He requires relaxation. He must resist the pressure to work night and day. He must not become obsessed. His fatherly duties come first. He must respect his peace of mind by protecting his tranquility. Mental tranquility is everything. Without it, he'll crumble. With it, he'll soar. Michael has every intention of soaring.

To maintain emotional balance, he has decided to turn his attention, at least for now, to the suite of classical music he has been composing for well over a year. Today he is meeting an orchestrator.

Composer-conductor David Michael Frank arrives at the Carolwood estate not knowing what to expect. When Michael appears dressed in black, Frank is cautious about shaking his hand. He has heard that Michael is germophobic. But there's no hesitancy on Michael's part. His handshake is robust. To Frank's eyes, the singer appears thin but fit.

Michael recognizes Frank from when they worked together on a TV tribute to Sammy Davis Jr. at the Shrine Auditorium in the winter of 1989. Michael sang a song of heartfelt appreciation, "You Were There," to the ailing entertainer, who would die a few months later.

Frank listens as Michael explains that he's simultaneously working on three projects: the tour, new pop songs, and an album of classical music. It's the classical music that requires Frank's help.

Before they get to work, Michael wants to discuss music. Frank senses that the singer is hungry for intellectual dialogue. Michael mentions his love of Aaron Copland's compositions, especially *Rodeo*, *Fanfare for the*

Common Man, and *Lincoln Portrait*. He also mentions the music written by Leonard Bernstein for the film version of *West Side Story*. Frank wonders if Michael also knows Bernstein's score for *On the Waterfront*. Michael does. A friend of the film's star, Marlon Brando, Michael has watched the movie several times.

The talk turns from Leonard to Elmer Bernstein. The minute Frank names *The Magnificent Seven* his favorite Elmer score, Michael starts singing the theme. As the music talk continues, Prince and Paris wander in and out of the room. Exhortations of "I love you, Daddy," "I love you, Paris," "I love you, Prince" reverberate.

Paris finds her father a CD player so Frank can hear Michael's work in progress. The instrumental music is ethereal and highly melodic. Michael explains that he needs Frank's help with some incomplete sections.

They move from the main house to the pool house, where a piano is situated. As Frank sits at the keyboard, Michael hums one of the missing sections. Frank provides the harmonic structure under Michael's melody.

"Your instincts are totally right about the chords," Michael tells Frank.

Frank is impressed with Michael's perfect pitch. For several minutes, the two musicians weave together their constructions, all the while capturing the sounds on Frank's digital tape recorder. Each piece is from seven to ten minutes long. To Frank's ears, one suggests an Irish origin; another has the feeling of John Barry's score for *Out of Africa*. Each bears the mark of a mature composer.

Michael is delighted with Frank's suggestions for bringing the music to fruition: the use of Celtic harps, the orchestration of a full string ensemble, the establishment of Michael's melodies against countermelodies.

Before the session is over, Michael again stresses how these compositions are close to his heart. It is his lifelong wish to write beyond the categories in which he has previously worked.

Michael walks Frank to the door and thanks him for his time. He assures Frank that their writing sessions will continue. Meanwhile, Frank will begin writing arrangements and suggests that they set up a recording date at one of the big movie studios. Would Michael have someone call about arranging a budget? Michael readily agrees.

A few weeks later, Michael calls Frank to ask if he's making progress. Frank says that he is, but he still hasn't heard from anyone in Michael's camp. Michael reassures him that someone will be in touch. He reasserts his wish that this new music be as beautiful as Debussy's Arabesque no. 1, a piece he has committed to memory. He also mentions a jazz composition he has recently completed.

Given Michael's hectic rehearsal schedule, Frank suggests that they record these pieces in London when the This Is It shows are over. Michael concurs.

The idea lingers in Michael's mind. It isn't merely that he seeks recognition beyond his role as pop star. Classical and jazz melodies have been haunting him for years. He cannot escape their lure. Music does not simply amuse or divert Michael; it pursues him. The motifs preoccupying his mind have been there since he was a child. The preoccupation can be a source of pleasure or exasperation, depending upon the theme. If Michael feels victimized, for example, his method is to extricate himself through song. Take "D.S.," the song from *HIStory* that attacks Tom Sneddon, the Santa Barbara district attorney who for twelve years unsuccessfully struggled to take Michael down. Written after the initial accusations in 1993 but before the trial in 2005, "D.S." is Michael's method of purging his rage. Sneddon, fictionalized as "Dom Sheldon," is characterized as a "cold man." Michael imagines D.S. in cahoots with the CIA and the KKK, an insanely zealous prosecutor who will go to any length to get his man, dead or alive. On this track, a restrained rhythm and blues guitarist will not do. Michael employs Slash, the gunslinger guitarist from Guns N' Roses, to decapitate his opponent.

Michael's only effective weapon is his music. He is not a forceful speaker or a convincing polemicist. In Live from Neverland Valley, his famous 1993 television appearance, he explained his recent rehab for pain pill addiction and the "horrifying experience" of being scandalized by the "incredible, terrible mass media" for publicizing the false allegations against him. At the start, he said that "I am doing well and I am strong," but the sight of Michael — seated before the camera in an open-collar red shirt, his hair askew, his face a whiter shade of pale — was hardly reassuring. His testimony felt forced and overwrought. Watching him, one had the feeling that he'd have been far more convincing had he sung a song about his predicament.

The songs of his innocence — "Childhood," for instance, which like "D.S." is from *HIStory* — perhaps do far more to win us over than any prepared statements. And, while Michael is not the author of "Man in the Mirror," when he performs that song, we believe that he is genuinely self-reflective and self-critical.

Self-consciousness, though, never impedes Michael's creative process. As a pure artist, he is possessed. He has no choice but to express the sounds inside his head. He must write. During his darkest days — alone in Moscow, exiled in Arabia, isolated in Ireland — music is always his way out. The music never stops. And if now, in the spring of 2009, music is renewing his spirit, he is doubly grateful for the fact that the music has assumed a wordless shape. He has lived through enough stories. In his songs he has told enough tales. He is delighted to be composing motifs free of narrative form. His classical and jazz pieces are about feelings unrelated to events. They are about pure joy, an emotional state that has long eluded him. To remain in this state is Michael's purpose in connecting with David Michael Frank. When Frank says that when they record he will be using a baton that once belonged to Leonard Bernstein, Michael, who once met the late maestro, is thrilled.

If there was only a way to forgo the impending series of shows and devote himself entirely to making music without considering the marketplace! No thought of sales! No worries about breaking records! No anxiety about being considered irrelevant and out of fashion!

Yet anxiety follows Michael like a recurring ailment for

which there seems to be no cure. Anxiety about the heavy schedule of rehearsals. Anxiety about the upcoming dates. Anxiety about the way he feels and the way he looks.

For these all-important dates — these super-critical comeback concerts — he must look better than at any time in his life. That's why the Botox treatments are so crucial. Botox will erase any trace of aging, mask any imperfections, and give him the confidence to reintroduce himself to his army of fans. Botox will also keep him from being soaked in sweat after each dance number. He can't stop getting Botox.

On Monday, May 4, and Tuesday, May 5, he goes back to Dr. Arnold Klein's office for more dermatological treatments and more Demerol — three hundred milligrams each day — to dull the pain. On Wednesday, May 6, the Demerol is reduced to two hundred milligrams. For eight weeks, since March 12, Michael has been injected with heavy-duty Botox and Botox-related medicines; it is also for eight weeks that he has been fed a steady diet of extraordinarily high doses of Demerol.

If his mind was clearer, perhaps he could work with David Michael Frank again. If his mind was clearer, perhaps he could begin attending rehearsals more consistently. If his mind was clearer, perhaps he could meet with management to make certain that his interests were being protected.

Instead, after these long and exhausting treatments at Klein's office, his energy is sapped. It's enough to go home and be with the kids. Enough to insulate himself in the cocoon of the Carolwood estate. Enough to select a film with the charm to captivate his heart and soul, a film with the power to turn his mind from his own problems to the problems of a fictional character, a character whom he can shower with love and affection.

One such character is Antoine Doinel, hero of François Truffaut's 1959 classic, *The 400 Blows*, an autobiographical treatment of the director's troubled childhood. Michael counts it among his favorite films. He returns to it in the privacy of the lush screening room, with the knowledge that it will comfort him. Comfort comes in the form of Truffaut's extraordinary empathy for children. Like the director himself, Michael feels deeply for Antoine, with his inability to adjust to a life controlled by callous adults: uncaring teachers, insensitive parents, apathetic neighbors. Michael identifies with the desperate loneliness that sits at the heart of Truffaut's central character. As a child commanded by his father, surrounded by his brothers, and adored by his fans, Michael nonetheless felt isolated and misunderstood. Like Antoine Doinel, he walked through the world as an alien.

Even today he feels suffocated by an odd sense of estrangement. He wants to reengage with the world. That's what this upcoming series of shows is all about. He wants to reengage with his family and fans. But he also fears the consequences of doing so, of falling back into the vortex of hyperactivity—the concerts, the praise, the attacks, the ungodly amount of scrutiny—that alienates him from normal life.

So he clings to his children. He withdraws into the absolute closest unit—his own nuclear family of four—hoping that, inspired by films like *The 400 Blows,* he will find the strength to venture back out and reassert his auto-biographical art, his release from the pressures that continue to make his inability to sleep a diurnal nightmare.

17

Vulnerable Today, Ruthless Tomorrow

By the end of the first week of May of 2009, Michael faces two grim developments.

His former manager Raymone Bain, who also served as his public relations liaison during the 2005 trial, files a suit against him in Washington, DC, for $44 million. Bain managed Michael in 2006 and 2007. It was she who initially introduced him to AEG, although at the time of that first meeting with the company's Randy Phillips — early 2007 — Michael expressed no interest in touring. Now that Michael has agreed to perform, Bain is demanding 10 percent of the AEG deal.

Another lawsuit is brought, this one from actress Ola Ray, who appeared as Michael's love interest in the video for "Thriller." Ray is contending that she is owed royalties from that video. Earlier in 2009, John Landis, the video's director and cowriter, also sued Michael for back royalties.

Meanwhile, of all those managers courting Michael, Frank Dileo, with his wily strategy, has been most effective. After Leonard Rowe — and his hookup with Patrick Allocco, who was behind AllGood Entertainment's Jacksons reunion concert — reestablished a close rapport with Joseph and Katherine and subsequently Michael, Dileo courted Rowe and Allocco in opposing AEG. He further aligned himself with Michael's parents in their opposition to Tohme Tohme. But when it looked as though the AEG O_2 concert contract was a lock and Michael had no interest in the reunion date, Dileo switched sides, dropping Rowe/Allocco and assuring AEG that he and he alone had Michael's ear. It wasn't long before Dileo was working out of the AEG office.

Because Dileo knows the artist so well, he is especially sensitive to those times when Michael cannot focus on managerial matters. That's when he moves in. Early May is such a time. Michael's passivity — or exhaustion — creates a space that Dileo quickly occupies.

"Frank Dileo was a great operator," said Walter Yetnikoff, his former boss, in 2014. "Michael recognized Frank's ability to get things done. If Frank was ruthless — as any good showbiz manager needs to be — well, hell, so much the better. Michael has a ruthless streak himself."

"Michael is the kind of guy who's absolutely vulnerable today and ruthless tomorrow," claimed Greg Phillinganes, the brilliant pianist-composer-arranger who worked on many of Michael's major projects. "I don't mean that he's hypocritical — he's not. He simply has these two sides to him. His ultrasensitivity is real. He's not simply sensitive to himself, but to others. I remember when he first began approaching me to tour with him. It was while we were in the studio recording *Bad*. In that sweet high-pitched voice of his, he'd walk by my keyboards and say, 'Hey, Greg, you like performing live, don't you?' I'd say, 'Yes,' and then he'd move on. Next day he might say, 'Hey, Greg, I hear you like touring. Is that right?' 'Sure,' I'd respond. But then another two or three weeks would go by before he'd actually come out and ask me to join his upcoming tour. Eventually, when he asked me to be his musical director, it was with that same tentative tone. I interpreted it two ways. First, he sincerely didn't want to impose upon my professional life. He wanted to make sure touring was something I genuinely wanted. And secondly, I believe he spoke so tentatively because he didn't want to be rejected. To avoid hearing me say no, he made it easy for me to avoid committing.

"I've always thought his ruthless side came out in the famous story about him and Paul McCartney. One day he's hanging out with Paul, who's taking him under his wing and schooling him about the great value of music publishing. And then, like lightning, Michael has struck a deal to buy the Beatles' catalog, much to Paul's chagrin.

"On a much smaller scale, I got a taste of Michael's methodology when he called me to write with him. This was at the end of the seventies, during the *Off the Wall* sessions. I went to the small studio he had on Hayvenhurst, when he was still living with his parents. He said, 'I have this song, but it's missing a part.' The song turned out to be 'Don't Stop 'Til You Get Enough.' I wrote the part quickly. Michael loved what I'd done and said that it pulled the whole song together. Silently, I tried to figure out what percentage of the song I had just written. Perhaps a third. But I didn't want to sound greedy, so when Michael asked me what my contribution might be worth, I said, 'Ten percent.' He agreed. For weeks afterward, I was walking on air. I had collaborated with Michael Jackson!

"Before the record came out, though, I got a call from Michael's manager. 'In reviewing that song,' he said, 'Michael has concluded that you really didn't write anything, but rather, you merely helped him arrange it. Therefore, there's no writing credit and no royalties.' You can imagine how I was crushed. I thought of going directly to Michael, but I didn't. Michael hates confrontations and I couldn't see myself cornering him.

"The only other time I wished I had spoken directly to Michael was during the Dangerous tour. We were in Dublin, on our way to London, and I was unhappy with the music. It wasn't up to par. The concerts were raggedy. That may be because Michael was struggling with his demons and had problems focusing. Because I loved Michael and really cared about his show, I wanted to speak to him. I wanted to tell him how critical it was to tighten up the presentation. I pressed security to get me a meeting. They promised that they'd get Michael on the phone and had me wait in my hotel room. The call never came. Later, I learned Michael was out shopping for toys. I dragged myself through several more shows, including Bucharest and

Tokyo, but I was drained. Michael had insulated himself from me, his own musical director. My spirit was depleted and I never toured with him again."

On May 8, 2009, Michael's spirit may be revived by the fact that, at long last, AEG has formally agreed to hire Dr. Conrad Murray as his personal doctor. Michael is comforted by the fact that Murray has begun to spend the night at the Carolwood estate. Unlike registered nurse Cherilyn Lee, Murray is willing to administer propofol. In fact, Murray will soon place his third order for the drug, along with several benzodiazepine medicines, with a pharmacy service in Las Vegas.

The absence of an anesthesiologist does not deter either Michael or Murray. They have never reconnected with Dr. David Adams, the anesthesiologist they met in Vegas, either because he was too expensive or because they have decided he isn't necessary.

When it comes to reducing the trauma surrounding his sleep, Michael is in no mood to take chances. He can no longer tolerate the all-night anxiety that comes with extreme insomnia. He cannot afford to have his days ruined by sleepless nights. He has to take action. And now that Murray is in his camp, he is certain that he will be given the right medicines to protect his precarious peace of mind.

On the morning of May 10, after a rough night during which the medicines apparently did little to promote his rest, Michael calls Murray. Michael sounds half-asleep, and

163

his words are alarmingly slurred. He speaks to his doctor about his grandiose ambition for London. The effect is unnerving, chilling, even ghostly.

"Elvis didn't do it," says Michael in an eerily despondent voice. "Beatles didn't do it. We have to be phenomenal. When people leave this show, when people leave my show, I want them to say, 'I've never seen nothing like this in my life. Go. Go...It's amazing. He's the greatest entertainer in the world.'"

Still barely coherent, in his drugged-out haze Michael describes his dream of a children's hospital. "I'm taking that money," he says, "a million children. A children's hospital, the biggest in the world. 'Michael Jackson's Children's Hospital.' Gonna have a movie theater, game room. Children are depressed...in those hospitals, no game room, no movie theater. They're sick because they're depressed. Their mind is depressing them. I want to give them that. I care about them, them angels. God wants me to do it...I'm gonna do it, Conrad."

Michael continues to reflect on his role as something of a savior. "Don't have enough hope," he says, speaking of young people. "That's the next generation that's gonna save our planet...My babies...They walk around with no mother. They drop them off, they leave—a psychological degradation of that. They reach out to me: 'Please take me with you.' I'm gonna do that for them. That will be remembered more than my performances. My performances will be up there helping my children and [will] always be my dream. I love them."

164

And here Michael repeats what he has convinced himself is the absolute essence of his psychological dilemma:

"I love them," he repeats, "because I didn't have a childhood. I had no childhood. I feel their pain. I feel their hurt. I can deal with it. 'Heal the World,' 'We Are the World,' 'Will You Be There,' 'The Lost Children.' These are the songs I've written because I hurt, you know, I hurt."

Countless times Michael has told himself—and the world—that he is the victim of a childhood-less life. This is the great narrative he has built up around himself. He believes it with all his heart. Because he has been forced to work—driven first by his father, and later by his own fierce ambition—he has been divested of what he fantasizes could have been a normal childhood. No carefree days playing in the park, no buddies from school, no kite flying or fishing in the stream, no strolling through the woods.

In Michael's mind, deprivation is tightly linked with entitlement. Or, as he wrote in his signature song "Childhood," it has been his "fate to compensate." What he didn't have then he must have now.

What he *did* have then was, of course, his family. However he might characterize his childhood (or lack thereof), during those early years he was not only surrounded by family; he was smothered by family. His family-centric beginnings formed his attitudes about everything. Once he got away from his family, he found the kind of freedom he had never known in childhood.

Yet his family, like his sense of childhood lost, is something he can neither forget nor escape.

18

Family Reunion

For Michael, his family of origin is a source of confusion. Love is mixed with skepticism, skepticism is mixed with nostalgia, nostalgia is mixed with reality, and reality is mixed with pain.

For over forty years, the Jacksons, raised in the public relations ethos of show business, have sugarcoated a wildly dysfunctional dynamic with a narrative that claims family unity above all.

As a child brutally teased by his brothers for his skin condition and less than manly mannerisms, Michael suffered deeply. In turn, he unmercifully teased his baby sister, Janet, about her weight and the size of her backside. Although Michael would later idealize children as the purest form of humanity, the truth was that he knew firsthand how cruel they could be.

He knew that adults could be even crueler. He watched Joseph mistreat Katherine by fathering a child outside their marriage. He viewed some of his brothers mirroring his father by mistreating their wives through long series of extramarital affairs. Watching his siblings, Michael saw marriage after marriage fall into ruins. In the eighties, he privately cited that very fact — the grave number of betrayals and ruined relationships he had seen in his own family — to explain his determination not to marry. And yet when he did marry, both of his marriages ended quickly and unhappily.

Consequently, on May 14, 2009, he arrives with profoundly mixed feelings at the surprise celebration of his parents' sixtieth wedding anniversary, orchestrated by sister Janet. The date of Katherine and Joseph's marriage was actually November 5, 1949. No one is quite sure why the party is taking place some six months earlier. But more troubling is the undisputed fact that Michael's parents have lived separate lives, in separate residences, even in separate cities, for decades. He wonders what, exactly, is being celebrated.

The answer, of course, is the idealized story sold to the press and embraced, at least at times like this, by the family itself. The story says that the Jacksons are all living happily ever after. It's a story that claims we're all for one and one for all, the same story that allows Michael to leave the isolation of the Carolwood estate and bring his children to a private room at Chakra, an Indian restaurant in Beverly Hills, so that they can mingle with their grandparents, uncles, aunts, and cousins.

For most of the Jacksons, this is the first time they have seen Michael since he left the country after the 2005 trial.

During the years that he sojourned in the Middle East and Ireland and subsequently settled in Las Vegas, before coming to Los Angeles to prepare for the London shows, he has kept his family at arm's length. Although the various members supported him during his legal nightmare, he pulled back from his family.

"His family saw him as the goose that laid the golden egg," said Bob Jones. "A long time ago — as early as the eighties — Michael had lost patience trying to solve the money woes of his parents and brothers. Like his song says, he wanted to be left alone."

But he also wants his children to feel that they do, in fact, belong to a large and loving dynasty. When four generations of Jacksons come together in the name of family solidarity, there is an undeniable feeling of goodwill and mutual support. Who is Michael to deny Prince, Paris, and Blanket such a warm and nurturing experience? Why shouldn't his kids enjoy the emotional benefits of being part of a large community of loving relatives?

The idea of one big happy family might be a myth, but it is a myth, on an evening such as this, that Michael can't resist. Besides, his siblings are people with tremendous natural charm. He loves seeing Janet and La Toya, with whom, at various times in his life, he has been extraordinarily close. Jackie, Tito, Marlon — they're all smiles, bubbling with enthusiasm about finally getting everyone together. Jermaine is especially gracious, telling Michael how much he loves one of Michael's most enchanting songs, "Fly Away," which was eliminated from the *Bad* album. As

Jermaine sings Michael the background parts, Michael joins him in harmony.

Harmony prevails. Relatives that Michael has not seen in far too long bring a broad smile to his face. He loves seeing his nieces and nephews, many of whom — like Tito's children, Taj, Taryll, and TJ, who formed the singing group 3T — he personally helped in their private and professional lives.

There are the private jokes that he shares with Janet, the two giggling like schoolkids. There are warm hugs from the people who knew him first and knew him best. Some, like La Toya and Jermaine, are concerned that Michael is alarmingly thin, but he seems strong nonetheless. His sweet spirit is intact. His spirit is buoyed by the attention he receives. Michael cannot help but feel genuine love coming his way.

He is here for his family and his children, but mostly for his mother. He could not bear to disappoint her by staying away. His presence pleases her greatly. She is, after all, the powerful matriarch, the only member with the emotional authority to bring this disjointed family together. It is Katherine Jackson who has decided that, in spite of its bitter and acrimonious past, her marriage to Joe Jackson is still cause for celebration. And it is at this party that Michael is reminded that he is expected to attend a meeting tomorrow with his parents and their man, Leonard Rowe.

Just when Michael thought that Rowe was out of the picture, Rowe is back. Despite the dominance of Frank

Dileo, Rowe is still angling to manage Michael by producing a reunion concert that will bring financial rewards to the Jackson family.

The purported purpose of this evening is simply to affirm family love. And yet when the celebration is over, Michael is made to see that there is another agenda. That agenda — mixing family loyalty with business — has been operative since he was a child.

For this middle-aged man, nothing has changed.

The May 15 business meeting makes Michael exceedingly uncomfortable. The setting is a secluded bungalow at the Beverly Hills Hotel, where moguls and movie stars mingle among well-heeled tourists.

In Michael's mind, the goodwill of last night's family reunion is gone. Family fellowship has led to family obligation. Michael thought he was through with such obligations long ago, yet he sits, quietly and only half attentively.

At the table are Joseph and Katherine, Leonard Rowe, and AEG executives Randy Phillips and Paul Gongaware. Having learned about Rowe's latest end run, AEG is concerned that his plan will undermine the O_2 shows.

Rowe is concerned that AEG is cheating Michael. He accuses the promoters of scalping tickets for the London show and excluding Michael from the profits. Phillips denies the charges. Siding with Rowe, Joe is especially animated, loudly exclaiming that he will not stand by and see his son hoodwinked.

Rowe continues to push his plan: his backer, Patrick Allocco of AllGood Entertainment, is offering $30 million for a Jacksons reunion concert on July 3 at Texas Stadium, home of the Dallas Cowboys.

Michael is not interested, especially when the AEG execs explain that their deal is exclusive. Contractually, Michael cannot perform at any other venue until he has completed all fifty O_2 shows. That should conclude the meeting, but Joe is not through. Katherine pleads with her son to hear what his father has to say.

Together, Joe and Leonard make their case. On an hourly basis, Michael will make far more for this one reunion concert than for all his O_2 shows combined. Beyond that, he will be bailing out his family. Joe needs the money, and so do his brothers. Where's Michael's sense of loyalty?

Michael allows Randy Phillips to reassert the legal impossibility of mounting any concerts before London. The contract is ironclad.

If that's the case, Joe argues, then the least Michael can do is give him, his mother, and his brothers a cut of the AEG deal.

Michael's patience is exhausted. Angrily, he tells his father no—no, he will not make him a party to his AEG engagement; no, he will not participate in any reunion concert; and no, he will not rehire Rowe as his manager or promoter. What's more, Michael insists that his brothers issue a statement confirming the fact that there will be no reunion concert.

Three days later, on May 18, the Jacksons — Jackie, Tito, Marlon, and Randy — do just that. To head off any possibility of legal action brought by AllGood Entertainment against Michael for refusing to participate in a reunion concert, the brothers now publicly claim that no such offer was ever made to them. They separate themselves entirely from AllGood. They wholeheartedly support Michael in his refusal to perform at Texas Stadium and wish him the best for his upcoming This Is It dates in London.

Seeing that Michael is adamant about being left alone to concentrate on the task before him — getting ready for London — the family finally backs off. But they are not happy.

Neither is Michael. The struggle for his mind has drained his soul. Although he ultimately rejects the argument that AEG is cheating him, those accusations resonate with his own previous doubts. He does, in fact, feel exploited — not just by AEG, but by everyone. He's still uncertain about the jump from ten to fifty shows. And, although it's been explained to him over and over again that his financial stability — plus the acquisition of Prince Jefri's dream mansion in Vegas — cannot be realized without the full complement of performances, he remains skeptical. No matter: he will send a letter to Rowe, clearly stating that Rowe is not his manager and that he, Michael, wants no part of a Jacksons reunion show.

Yet as he leaves the Beverly Hills Hotel, Michael remains riddled with equivocation. He feels both relief and regret at separating himself from his family — relief from

173

the pressure of monetarily supporting them, and regret that the love and warmth from last night's reunion has so quickly dissipated. He is also disquieted by the fact that his future is in the hands of people about whom he harbors grave doubts.

Confusion returns. Confusion remains. Confusion clouds his mind as he wonders, *Who do I trust? When do I trust? How do I trust?*

Confusion follows him as his entourage, pursued relentlessly by the ever-present paparazzi, snakes its way through Beverly Hills before arriving at the offices of Dr. Arnold Klein.

Then another feeling, this one generated by an injection of Demerol, replaces confusion. The new feeling — an old feeling — is, at least temporarily, a good feeling, a feeling that allows him to float above it all.

But when that good feeling dissolves and evening comes, confusion returns and is only defeated when Michael drifts off, with the assistance of Dr. Murray and the nightly dose of propofol, the milky substance that finally allows him to disappear deep, deep, deep into the dark comfort of dreamless sleep.

19

Elvis

Just as Michael has studied the lives of Jesus Christ, P. T. Barnum, Charlie Chaplin, Walt Disney, and Fred Astaire, he has carefully studied the life of Elvis Presley. Even before marrying Elvis's daughter, Michael was obsessed with Elvis's myth. He relates to Elvis as an artist with working-class roots whose rise to icon status revolutionized popular culture. With the exception of the Beatles—who were, after all, a quartet, not a solo act—Michael became the biggest artist since Elvis. Like Elvis, Michael grew up in the throes of fundamentalist Christianity. And like Elvis, Michael wandered away from his church, seeking spiritual paths with an Eastern bent. Elvis also battled with prescription drugs.

On this May morning, a few hours before Michael is due to return to Dr. Klein's office, he thinks about Elvis's search for a peace of mind that he could never find. Michael has read about how the prescription medicines both helped and hurt Elvis. He remembers reading statements by

Priscilla, Elvis's former wife, about the doctors Elvis controlled and the spiritual guides he met.

Through his hairdresser, Elvis was introduced to a number of books — *Siddhartha,* by Hermann Hesse; *The Prophet,* by Kahlil Gibran; *Autobiography of a Yogi,* by Paramahansa Yogananda — that Michael himself has read. Priscilla described Elvis's visit to the Self-Realization Fellowship Lake Shrine in Pacific Palisades, a few miles west of the Carolwood estate. It was there that Elvis heard the name Sri Daya Mata, the woman who became the spiritual leader of the self-realization community after the death of Yogananda. Later, Elvis and Priscilla drove up Mount Washington to meet Sri Daya Mata, called "Ma" by her followers. The words she said to Elvis resonate with Michael. When Elvis admitted that he wanted a crash course in spirituality, when he said he was in a hurry to achieve a higher state of mind, Sri Daya Mata explained that, when it comes to matters of the soul, there are no shortcuts. Spiritual evolution is a slow process. It takes months, years, decades. Patience is needed. Patience is mandatory. Without patience, there's no progress. With patience, change is certain.

Michael knows the rest of the Elvis story all too well. The Colonel, Elvis's Machiavellian manager, saw his client's spiritual search as a threat to the financial well-being of everyone in the Elvis camp. Because Elvis, like Michael, was vulnerable to managerial manipulations, he was easily sidetracked. The Colonel quickly put a stop to what he perceived as Elvis's seduction by mumbo jumbo. He cut off communication between Elvis and the guru. The Colonel couldn't afford to have anyone mess with his client's mind.

Michael's mind goes back to Deepak Chopra, one of the several wise men with whom he has consulted over the years. Michael met Chopra — world-renowned author, meditation teacher, and holistic physician — back in the late eighties. It was Chopra, a favorite of Oprah Winfrey, who introduced Michael to meditation, Sufi poetry, and the works of the Bengali literary light Rabindranath Tagore. Later, Chopra's son, Gotham, worked with Michael on the Dangerous tour. It was also through Chopra that Michael met and hired nanny Grace Rwaramba.

Michael didn't merely seek spiritual advisors; he sought gurus who, like himself, had achieved international notoriety. He courted, in addition to celebrated meditation teachers, the company of famous magicians like David Blaine and David Copperfield. The latter was set to work on the This Is It shows until he priced himself out of Michael's range.

Michael often dreamed of combining magic and meditation. He was intrigued, for example, by the notion of levitation. He loved all phenomena that challenged and altered reality.

"I once told Michael that the purpose of the artist is to reveal those unknown worlds that exist beyond our mortal perceptions," said Marvin Gaye. "I said that the true artist must lift the veil of surface reality. Michael knew just what I was talking about."

A seeker of the deepest reality, Deepak Chopra acted as editor and ghostwriter for Michael's 1992 collection of poems, short stories, and meditations, *Dancing the Dream*. Sold as a souvenir during the Dangerous tour, the book, replete with dozens of photos of Michael, deals with the themes of love, courage, and magic. Most prominent are the subjects of underprivileged children and the pain of lost childhood. In writing about lost children, Michael is essentially writing about himself. Compared to his days as a believing Jehovah's Witness, his theology now is radically transformed to the point that he envisions God as a woman. He sees "her" in the glow of a rainbow, the beauty of a deer, and the affection of a father. In what is either a Freudian typo or an intentional play on words, the book is "Deicated to Mother with love." A poem that Michael includes called "Mother" does, in fact, deify Katherine as a faultless angel.

Just as Michael turned to Chopra for one sort of wisdom, he looked to Rabbi Shmuley Boteach for another. The idea of having a personal spiritual guide had enormous appeal to Michael, whose sense of altruism battled his sense of entitlement.

At this time—the third week in May—Michael knows full well that he is entitled to look and feel his best. Elvis experimented with prescription drugs until the experiments turned bad, but that was over thirty years ago. Medicine has evolved. Medicine has improved. Dermatology has improved. Over decades, Michael has learned an enormous amount about medicine, especially dermatological care. He knows which drugs and treatments work for him and which do not. He also knows how to compartmentalize the various treatments he receives. For instance, Conrad Murray, his at-home primary physician, is not advised about the heavy doses of Demerol that Michael is getting from Arnold Klein multiple times a week. Meanwhile, Michael sees no reason to tell Klein that Murray is now sedating him with propofol on a nightly basis.

Michael feels best when he is in control. Just as he is able to manage his music, his choreography, and his total stage presentation, he can manage his health.

His health is of great concern to AEG. Seeing how many rehearsals Michael has missed and how unfocused he appears, the promoters decide to push back the first This Is It show from July 8 to July 13. That gives him eight weeks to get ready.

The new start date is a relief. Michael can finally exhale. He knows that these extra five days are exactly what he needs. When it comes to the big performance, he will be ready. He is programmed to rise to the occasion. He sees a clear path ahead. Right now, though, that path leads back to the offices of Arnold Klein. On three consecutive days—May 19, 20, and 21—Michael revisits the doctor for an assortment of skin treatments and his steady dose of Demerol.

Somewhere in the drug-induced twilight zone, Michael moves back and forth between a carefree world where everything is falling into place and a world where everything is falling apart.

Now he is cheerful and ebullient. His children are by his side. His children are safe, beautiful, well behaved, a tribute to their loving father. They are sheltered in a spacious estate, guarded by highly trained security professionals, given books and games and films to nourish their minds.

But soon his cheerfulness leads to anxiety about the rehearsals he's missing and the looming commitment to entertain the world in London. The shows must be magical. For a few fleeting seconds, he can see the magic in his mind's eye. He pictures the opening number, "Wanna Be Startin' Somethin'." He stands on a pitch-dark stage. Above him is a globe made of glass. The globe will slowly start to turn, floating around his body before moving out into the audience, glowing like a comet—flitting here, flitting there, flitting everywhere. And then, with a graceful extension of his arm, Michael beckons the luminous globe. Like a shooting star, it zooms back to the stage and lands in Michael's open hand, where, in a burst of radiant colors, it explodes, its fragments disappearing into the night.

Michael sees the show continuing. Somewhere in the middle of the performance, there's nothing onstage except a mattress set on fire. The groove drops on "Dirty Diana," a song from *Bad* that describes the exploits of a desperate groupie lurking by the backstage door with hopes of seducing a superstar like Michael. Diana is cast as an erotic pole dancer who, whenever her feet touch the stage, sends up shooting flames. She pursues Michael with fierce purpose. Her weapons are gilded ropes that, for all his evasive moves, seem to ensnare and bind Michael to the bedposts of the burning bed. A red diaphanous curtain descends. Michael has been caught, apparently tied up like captured prey. But then the curtain rises to reveal a plot twist: it isn't Michael who's tied up like captured prey — it's Dirty Diana. Michael has triumphed once again.

When Michael conveys these ideas to Ed Alonzo, a magician who is helping to create some of the show's most spectacular stage moments, it is with the exhortation that these illusions stun and stir his fans to the point of frenzy. Michael wants the audience to be caught in a hysterical state of wonder and delight.

He wants to live in a state of wonder and delight. To do so, Michael knows that it's best to avoid the news. He doesn't want to hear about the suicide bombings in Iraq, the mutilation in Somalia, or the devastation in Afghanistan. These are situations that baffle Michael. He can't comprehend why — in the name of love — murderous ethnic animosity can't come to an end. Even more baffling are natural disasters like earthquakes and floods that kill hundreds of thousands of people.

If God is all-loving and all-powerful, why does he allow — or even cause — the loss of innocent life, especially the deaths of helpless children? Why does God tolerate political slaughter? This is a question that Michael has posed to all the gurus he has sought for comfort.

"Why didn't something in heaven stop the Holocaust or some of the great genocides that happen in the world, from the lynchings and slavery to all the great problems?" he once asked Rabbi Boteach.

The usual answers—that God is enigmatic, that his ways cannot be known, that we must live on faith—only partially satisfy Michael. Yet he cannot imagine himself not believing in God. He has always believed in the Great Creator. When he looks at the glorious wonders of the world—the mountains and forests and deserts and oceans—or at the majesty of space—the stars and constellations, the galaxies within galaxies—his heart says that they are all God's handiwork. How can it be otherwise?

On one hand, unanswered questions. On the other hand, undeniable evidence.

As an adult, Michael has concluded that, unlike when he embraced fundamentalist theology as a child, he must now live with uncertainty. That is an uncomfortable conclusion. He would love to return to an earlier conviction, a time when all the answers were spelled out, and the fate of the world—as well as his own soul—was made clear. That's no longer possible.

In what he has called his favorite song, "Earth Song," the hymn from *HIStory*, Michael does more than pose a series of questions about the ways in which man has mutilated his environment. He also confronts the Christian God, the one who has pledged his "only son" to a world of peace. Michael bravely asks God whether he really cares about the dying dreams and the atrocity of "children dead from war."

In "Earth Song," often called Michael's most stirring anthem, the questions resonate, without answers. God remains distant, silent, unknowable.

Having lived for half a century, all Michael knows is that the struggle continues: the struggle to protect the planet; the struggle to protect his children and himself; the struggle to satisfy his enormous material needs and material obsessions; the struggle to please everyone around him, including his family and fans; and the struggle to locate enough peace of mind to assure him the rest of a blameless child.

20

Do or Die

Sunday, May 31, 2009

Michael knows that there's a big, splashy article about him in the *Los Angeles Times.* He knows this because, even though his advisors are careful not to hand him newspapers and magazines that treat him critically, he spends a great deal of time on the Internet. In addition to doing his eBay shopping, for which he buys impulsively with a variety of pseudonymous accounts, he cannot resist reading about himself, especially critiques that appear in major publications.

The *Times* piece, an attempt to assess Michael's current situation some six weeks before the This Is It kickoff concert in London, focuses on Tom Barrack, the billionaire who bailed out Michael over a year ago and brought in AEG. Barrack is optimistic, telling the paper that Michael "could make $500 million a year if he puts his mind to it."

Although the article's tone is mostly upbeat, there are

quotes that bother Michael. One is from his former lawyer, John Branca, who says, "The paradox is that Michael is one of the brightest and most talented people I've ever known. At the same time, he has made some of the worst choices in advisors in the history of music." The lawyer characterizes his separation from the singer as his own choice, not Michael's.

Randy Phillips of AEG tells the paper about initially approaching Michael in 2007, when the artist "wasn't ready" to realize a comeback. But now that he is ready, there is also a proposal for a three-year tour after London, going from Europe to Asia to the United States. Michael's sole commitment is the fifty O_2 concerts, but clearly AEG is hoping for much more.

"We could have done two hundred shows if he were willing to live in London for two years," says Phillips.

Reading the remainder of the article, in which there is talk of risk, makes Michael uncomfortable. AEG is paying more than $20 million to produce the concerts—double the original estimate—and of the fifty performances, the promoter has been able to secure insurance for only twenty-three. "In this business," says Phillips, "if you don't take risks, you don't achieve greatness."

When asked about Michael's health, Phillips says that the artist has passed "a rigorous medical examination."

Things get murky when Tohme Tohme again identifies himself as Michael's manager and speaks of the benefits of the association with Barrack and AEG, while implying that past advisors were less than scrupulous.

But when Frank Dileo speaks to the paper, he assures readers that *he* is in charge and that Tohme Tohme has been dismissed.

Furthermore, Cannon & Company, the accounting firm hired by Michael in 2008, has reportedly also been fired.

There's mention of other figures, some considered suspect, who have reemerged to either boost Michael's confidence or cash in on his comeback, depending upon one's point of view.

The article's implication is plain: Michael's camp is in disarray. Among those weighing in on the high drama of his business affairs, the only two characters who speak with convincing authority are the supreme moneymen: Tom Barrack and Randy Phillips. And it is Phillips who underlines the article's central theme. "The concerts, Phillips acknowledged, are a do-or-die moment for Jackson," writes the paper, before quoting Phillips directly: "If it doesn't happen, it would be a major problem for him career-wise in a way that it hasn't been in the past."

Michael perceives this as a warning. Phillips is unhappy that Michael has missed so many rehearsals and is warning him about the consequences. Warnings do not please Michael. Warnings do not motivate him. They anger him. The idea of a "do-or-die moment" does not sit well with him. Why should he, of all people, be threatened by promoters who stand to make millions off him?

That phrase — "do-or-die" — haunts him through the day and into the evening. It is Sunday, Murray's day off. The doctor will not be there to give him the "milk of amnesia" that knocks him out. That means taking other medicines and hoping against hope that they will work.

Bone-weary, Michael struggles to renew his sense of hope, a precious commodity that, night after night, slips away.

21

How Did It Get
So Late So Soon?

The words from Dr. Seuss, one of Michael's favorite writers, are both apt and sad: "How did it get so late so soon? / It's night before it's afternoon. / December is here before it's June."

June has arrived in a mad rush. Things are changing overnight. Everyone is in a hurry to make sure these shows come off.

On June 1, rehearsals move from CenterStaging, the facility in Burbank where the ten-thousand-square-foot soundstage can no longer accommodate the colossal production, to the Forum, in Inglewood.

The next day chef Kai Chase is rehired by the man who fired her, Michael Amir. Just as no reason was given for her dismissal, no reason is given for her recommission. Having been absent from the Carolwood estate for one month, she is shocked by the difference in Michael's demeanor. Four weeks ago, he seemed energetic and strong. Now he appears lethargic and weak.

Grace Rwaramba has resurfaced in London, where she claims to be once again working for Michael, this time scouting out a house for him and the children to live in for the duration of the This Is It shows. There's no indication from Michael that Grace has, in fact, been rehired.

Meanwhile, Michael remains preoccupied with his frail health and his need to sleep. He continues his practice of seeing other physicians—Allan Metzger and plastic surgeon Larry Koplin—who reportedly refuse to give him the powerful drugs he seeks.

Concerned about Michael's visits to so many doctors and his absence from rehearsals, Randy Phillips of AEG comes to Carolwood, where he, his assistant Paul Gongaware, Frank Dileo, Conrad Murray, and Michael discuss the current state of the artist's health. The meeting is tense. Michael makes it clear to Phillips, the moneyman, that everything is cool. While it's true that he has missed many rehearsals, he reminds the group that he has been diligently working on his dance routines on a daily basis at home with choreographer Travis Payne. Michael has it under control. He knows the schedule. He knows what needs to be done. And he knows how to do it.

A few days earlier, when he was leaving CenterStaging, he didn't sound as confident. Addressing a number of fans, he was visibly upset when he said, "I don't know how I'm going to do fifty shows. I'm not a big eater. I need to put some weight on. I'm really angry with them [for] booking me up to do fifty shows. I only wanted to do ten, and take the tour around the world to other cities, not fifty in one place. I went to bed knowing I sold ten dates, and woke up to the news that I was booked to do fifty."

It seemed as though that issue was already resolved. Now, on June 2, another issue that Michael thought was behind him is back in the news. Contrary to what Michael has written to Leonard Rowe, Rowe's backer, Patrick Allocco of AllGood Entertainment, is claiming that Michael is committed to a reunion concert. The promoter has complete confidence that, in his words, "the historic show we have been planning for more than a year" will be realized. Eight days later, though, Allocco changes course and, seeking to bar the upcoming This Is It shows in London, sues Michael and Frank Dileo, once an Allocco ally, for $20 million in lost profits and another $20 million in punitive damages.

Whether as a result of AEG's warnings or his own sense of responsibility, Michael begins attending rehearsals on a more regular basis. From June 1 through June 11, he never misses a day at the Culver Studios, where director Kenny Ortega is filming video adaptations of Michael's most famous songs, for use in the This Is It shows.

The high-tech wizardry—called the Dome Project—captures Michael's imagination. In reshaping "Smooth Criminal," he loves inserting himself into the film noirs of Edward G. Robinson and Humphrey Bogart. It's a way of re-creating the golden age of Hollywood, with Michael as the centerpiece of each story. His kids are there to watch the filming. Paris tells Ortega that this is the first time she's seen her father on a movie set. For his part, Michael is concerned that his children behave themselves—and they do. He's proud.

When he arrives home after working on these video adaptations, he feels renewed. He loves the filmmaking process. He relishes revisiting and resculpting videos, especially those made during the heady days of *Thriller*. He remembers that it was Quincy Jones, already a Hollywood star as a soundtrack composer and music producer, who introduced him to Steven Spielberg. Quincy and Michael were toiling away at *Thriller* at the same time that Spielberg was working on *E.T.* Both projects turned out to be among the most successful pop culture products of the twentieth century. Michael and Steven saw each other as magicians—one with music, the other with film. After Quincy produced and Michael narrated *E.T.: The Extra-Terrestrial*, the audiobook and soundtrack album on which Michael sang the theme song "Someone in the Dark," Steven and the artist became fast friends and for years spoke of making movies together.

Michael thinks back on those extravagant plans, all of them unrealized. He has never made a full-length feature. *Captain EO*, with its $30 million budget and groundbreaking technical innovations, was only seventeen minutes long. His idea to produce *Peter Pan*—and perhaps play the lead—remains, like most of his fantastical film projects, an unfulfilled dream. At the same time, he takes pride in the fact that the startlingly inventive nature of his short films has changed the course of pop music. In the early eighties, on the sheer strength of his phenomenal popularity, he broke the color barrier on MTV. As time went on, his videos had a distinctly autobiographical bent. While it's true that he hired distinguished directors, given the scope and cohesion of his cinematic work, Michael could easily be considered an auteur.

He also remembers the accolades he received for his acting. In "Bad," for example, the brilliant Martin Scorsese–directed video, he holds his own against a riveting Wesley Snipes. Michael plays a shy and studious ghetto kid who attends prep school on scholarship. In his first major screen appearance, Snipes plays a B-boy bully. To verify his manhood and authenticate his black identity, Michael must perform in urban street style. The proving ground is a Brooklyn subway station. "What are you going to do," asks Snipes, "dance us to death?" The answer is yes. In short order, Michael puts to death the myth that he is not black enough, not down enough, not daring or dangerous enough. Not only do his lock-and-pop moves have all the flash of the sharpest cutting-edge *Soul Train* dancers — some of whom, like Shalamar's Jeffrey Daniel, helped train him — but his assertion that first and foremost he is a soul singer has never been more convincing. When he scats the sound "shamone" over and over again, soul music fans immediately hear the reference to Sister Mavis, who employed that exact vocal filler in her rendition of the Staple Singers' sacred-secular pop hit from 1972 about the joys of heaven, "I'll Take You There."

Michael does, in fact, take us to a sacred place when the music stops and, in a scenario repeated in "Smooth Criminal," he breaks into a form of pure—or, better yet, impure—preaching. He and his dancers fall into a vignette of moans and cries, a deep call-and-response dialogue as old as the field shouts and primitive church services of nineteenth-century rural black America.

"Bad" allows Michael to realize an example of character development—from reticent nerd to artistic hero—that must be counted among his greatest achievements. Rivaling "Bad" as pure cinematic magic is his long-form video *Ghosts*, featuring the song by this name from *Blood on the Dance Floor*. That was twelve years ago, but Michael remembers it as if it were yesterday. Cowritten by Michael and Stephen King and directed by special effects master Stan Winston, it is Michael's most sinister and satisfying venture into gothic fantasy.

Michael plays the part of both the maestro and his adversary, the puffed-up mayor. The maestro, a surrogate for the real-life Michael, is the guardian of the haunted house that the rabidly reactionary mayor is determined to shut down. It is no accident that the mayor has the demeanor of Tom Sneddon, the prosecutor who pursued Michael with unchecked zeal. In perhaps the most transcendent moment in any Michael Jackson video, the mayor is consumed by the maestro's magic and, in an astonishing dance, expresses a range of rhythmic fury that seems to set him free of all animus. There is a skeletal dance—starring a disembodied Michael Jackson—that also carries the

194

suggestion of emotional catharsis. Michael is free of his enemies, free of his physical preoccupations, free to become nothing more than the form of his dance.

Michael sees film as a way to both escape and redefine reality—his ultimate fantasy. He has never lost his desire to become a master filmmaker himself. And now, looking back at the titans with whom he has worked—Spielberg, Scorsese, Coppola, Lucas, Winston—he feels that, in spite of every obstacle that came his way, he has made his mark in movies.

The truth is that he'd much rather be making a movie than preparing for months of grueling shows and, most likely, still another world tour. The fact that he has already done three world tours as a solo performer—Bad, Dangerous, and HIStory—doesn't ease his apprehension. Hundreds of dates in dozens of countries before millions of fans—those tours went on for years. When he is reminded that his only solo tour that came to the United States was Bad—and that was twenty-one years ago—he hears his promoters arguing the necessity of bringing This Is It back home. Their arguments center on one thing and one thing only: money. The money to pay off his debts, the money to buy the palatial estate in Las Vegas, the money to make the movies of his dreams.

"Price of Fame" pops into Michael's mind. It's one of the approximately fifty songs he wrote for *Bad* that never made it onto the album. Like dozens of his unreleased compositions—"Don't Be Messin' Round," "I'm So Blue," "Free," "Streetwalker," "Fly Away"—it stands as a remarkable work. The story centers on a warning issued by "Father":

if it's fortune and fame that you're after, your life will never be serene. That's the price of fame. You have no right to complain, no right to even feel the pain. If you do manage to escape—to a remote village, say—the world will soon forget about you. You can't run that risk. So live with it. This is the reality you've chosen. You can fashion your disguises, you can beef up your security, but you'll never escape. You'll always be found. You don't belong to yourself. You belong to the world. Don't think. Don't reflect. Your only job is to sign on the dotted line and perform.

To escape the traps of fame—to be "Free" or "Fly Away"—is merely wishful thinking, still another unfulfilled fantasy. Try as you might, you'll never stop paying the price for fame, because fame, for all the suffering it causes, is your cross, your obsession, your unalterable fate.

Michael thinks about the stories he read as a child; he also thinks about the stories he read as an adult seeking to deepen his understanding of life. The ones that moved him most—the stories of Jesus and Peter Pan and the Elephant Man and E.T. and Hamlet and the Greek god Dionysus—were all about the inevitability of fate.

Now, merely a month away from the start of the next major chapter in his whirlwind life, Michael wonders about his own fate.

What is it?

22

On the Good
Ship Lollipop

On Wednesday, June 10, Michael goes to Dr. Klein's office for the first time in six days. Before he leaves, he's given two hundred milligrams of Demerol.

Two days later, he makes an appearance at the Forum for a rehearsal, but his participation is limited. He's distracted and lethargic. It's difficult for Michael to concentrate on any of the routines. His security men explain to the press, which congregates in front of the rehearsal space, that, due to his extreme fatigue, Michael really doesn't want to be in the arena.

Fatigue is the reason given for his missing the next three straight days of rehearsals. AEG is more than concerned. The promoters are alarmed. Messages fly back and forth between them and Conrad Murray, who continues to claim that Michael is fine.

Michael is secluded at the Carolwood estate. For now, he is not working out with Lou Ferrigno, he is not practicing his dance routines, and he is not working on his music. Instead, he is looking for ways to comfort himself. To keep his thoughts from racing to the future, he lets his mind settle on the past. In the past, when he endured long periods of high anxiety, he relied on several methods to calm the emotional storms. For years—especially during those times when he was on the road—he insisted that his hotel bedroom be covered with pictures of Shirley Temple as a child star. For Michael, she is the personification of sweet innocence. Her image soothes his restless soul: the blond ringlets, the sparkling smile, the dimpled cheeks, the lilting little-girl voice, the bubbly personality. Michael knows all her movies, from *Bright Eyes* to *The Littlest Rebel* to *The Little Princess*. With great delight he listens to her sing "Animal Crackers in My Soup" and "On the Good Ship Lollipop." With even greater delight he watches the dazzling hoofer Bill "Bojangles" Robinson teach her to tap. Michael views Shirley Temple—just as he views Elizabeth Taylor in *National Velvet* and Judy Garland in *The Wizard of Oz* and Sammy Davis Jr. in *Rufus Jones for President*—as Hollywood royalty of the highest order, which is to say the youngest order. He sees himself in these child actors, their charm captured and frozen forever at a moment in their lives when their beauty was unspoiled.

Michael remembers when, as an adult, he went to meet the former child star who became the distinguished stateswoman Shirley Temple Black. He wept uncontrollably. In relating the experience to Rabbi Shmuley Boteach, Michael explained that he left her house feeling "baptized." He couldn't stop telling Shirley how merely looking at her little-girl image had saved him from utter despair. He let her know that for years a member of his staff had been assigned to turn his suites into Shirley Temple shrines, filling them with posters and life-sized cutouts. Worshipping at those shrines had kept him from, as he said, "throwing in the towel." Shirley responded with kindness, taking Michael's hand and saying that she understood, that she loved him. "I'm sorry I grew up," she apologized. The apology moved Michael to more tears. He too felt guilty for having grown up and desecrated the purity of his youth.

He remembers a story that he has told for decades, the one about a lady who recognized him and his brothers at the airport. At the time, Michael was in his teens.

"Are you the Jackson Five?" she asked.

"Yes," he answered.

"And where's cute little Michael?"

"I'm Michael."

The woman looked him over, made a face, and said in disgust, "What happened? Ugh!"

Michael thinks of what happened to the Our Gang kids and to Bobby Driscoll, the voice of Peter Pan and an Academy Juvenile Award–winning Disney child star who was featured in *Song of the South*, *So Dear to My Heart*, and *Treasure Island*, only to die a penniless drug addict in

1968, the year the Jackson 5 auditioned for Berry Gordy in Detroit.

He thinks of the pledge he made to Shirley Temple Black: to build and maintain a museum for child stars, the obscure as well as the famous, so that both their contributions and their suffering would never be forgotten. He wonders how he will represent himself in the museum. Will there be only pictures of the irresistibly cute preteen Michael? Will he be able to display photos from when his fourteen-year-old face, like Bobby Driscoll's, was ravaged with acne? Will he be able to look at images of himself from when he was trapped in those long and awkward stages of his postadolescent life, when he hated everything about his appearance? Will he be able to bear it?

The purpose of the museum would be to permanently capture the good feelings generated by the child stars. But how do you separate the good from the bad? When Michael sees a picture of himself as a young boy, he feels compelled—as did Shirley Temple Black—to apologize. "I'm sorry," he says to the world. But sorry for what? Sorry for growing up? Sorry for not being able to prolong the sweet innocence that charmed and comforted his fans? Sorry for developing into an artist compelled to incorporate anger and fear into his songs? Sorry for becoming a complicated and conflicted adult?

Sometimes when he listens to old Jackson 5 songs—the enduring hits like "ABC" or "The Love You Save"—he hears in his voice a fresh optimism and guileless joy that he hardly recognizes as his own. The silken smoothness of the voice continued into adolescence, into the seamless dance grooves of "Shake Your Body (Down to the Ground)" and "Off the Wall." He hears his voice darken and assume an edge of desperation when, on *Thriller*, he begins to explore unchartered territory in deeply personal songs like "Billie Jean." Because "Billie Jean" is an enormous hit, Michael sees that his fans are willing — even eager — to accompany him on his journey of self-exploration. The floodgates are opened, and Michael never looks back. His life becomes his art. His life becomes his songs, his videos, his dances. To express the confusion of his life, his voice necessarily becomes pained. His voice expresses the full range of his emotional contradictions: all at once he feels blessed, victimized, misunderstood, grateful, furious, brave, afraid, heroic, helpless, powerful, impotent, vulnerable, and invincible.

Now, on Tuesday, June 16, Michael feels increasingly disoriented and weak. It is far more than a physical fatigue. It is a mental fatigue, a spiritual fatigue. He thinks of a Marvin Gaye song from *What's Going On* that he has long loved, an ethereal meditation on escaping through chemicals called "Flyin' High (In the Friendly Sky)," in which the singer reflects on a world filled with folks who are "tired and weary." For relief, he goes to a place "where danger awaits." Michael knows that Marvin is talking about addicts and that, as in Michael's own testament to the power of drugs — "Morphine," from *Blood on the Dance Floor* — the subject is the allure of a drug-induced state.

Yet in Michael's mind the office of Dr. Arnold Klein is

not a place where danger awaits. Michael is not a street junkie. He is not a junkie at all. He is the patient of some of the world's most renowned physicians. His ongoing dermatological treatments are not indulgences. They are necessary. He cannot accept any plan other than one that allows him to retain the face of eternal youth. Anything else, any sign of deterioration, any indication of aging, will drive him mad. Images of Shirley Temple as a young girl, images of himself as a young boy — these are pictures that have remained unsoiled, the pictures to be treasured and preserved.

To preserve this picture is an arduous procedure. Demerol is the price that Michael pays. Demerol turns these treatments from pain into pleasure. On Tuesday, Demerol is the order of the day.

On Wednesday, June 17, Michael returns to rehearsals, where, according to his former lawyer, John Branca, he and Michael have an emotional reunion. It appears — at least to Branca — that after their long estrangement, he and Michael are back in business. Their rapprochement may well have been facilitated by Frank Dileo, who worked closely with Branca when they guided Michael through the wildly lucrative days of *Thriller* and *Bad*. If reinstating Branca means more stability for Michael, AEG has no complaints.

But AEG has other complaints, deadly serious complaints about the state of Michael's health. At this same June 17 rehearsal, an observer, shocked by the singer's appearance, says, "That's not Michael up there. He's like a ghost."

The next day, Thursday, June 18, Michael fails once again to show up for rehearsals at the Forum. In total frustration, director Kenny Ortega sends an email to AEG's Randy Phillips, suggesting that Michael's chronic absences from the rehearsals might mean that it's time to fold the tent and call it a day. Incensed, Phillips takes it upon himself to drive to Carolwood, where he somehow convinces Michael to get to rehearsal. He also confronts Conrad Murray about Michael's repeated visits to the office of Dr. Arnold Klein and the drugs that the artist has been ingesting. But Murray, like everyone else in the Jackson camp, has no control over Michael. In the word of Berry Gordy, Michael has become "rudderless."

Michael finally arrives at the Forum at around 10 p.m. and stays for several hours, but his participation is limited and his disorientation still disturbingly apparent.

It has been only a week since Michael was present for the Dome Project filming at the Culver Studios, where Ortega viewed the artist as an active and focused participant. Now Ortega is telling Phillips an entirely different story: that Michael is displaying "strong signs of paranoia, anxiety, and obsessive-like behavior…It's like there are two people there. One [deep inside] trying to hold on to what he was and still can be and not wanting us to quit him, the other in his weakened and troubled state."

The next day, Friday, June 19, Michael is even worse.

He makes it to the Forum but is unable to sing or dance. Kenny Ortega sends him home and emails Phillips that Michael "appeared quite weak and fatigued this evening. He had a terrible case of the chills, was trembling, rambling, and obsessing." Ortega goes on to say that he covered Michael in blankets and massaged his feet in an effort to assuage his anxiety. He's concerned that after Phillips played what Ortega calls the "tough love, now or never card," Michael "may be unable to rise to the occasion due to real emotional stuff." Ortega is further convinced that Michael needs to be "psychologically evaluated." "It would shatter him, break his heart if we pulled the plug," he goes on to say. "He's terribly frightened it's all going to go away. He asked me repeatedly tonight if I was going to leave him. He was practically begging for my confidence. It broke my heart. He was like a lost boy. There still may be a chance he can rise to the occasion if we get him the help he needs."

Saturday, June 20, the last day of rehearsals for the dancers at the Forum. Michael does not show up.

Home at the Carolwood estate, he seeks solace. His body is increasingly and inexplicably cold. It may be the meds; it may be the relentless assault of anxiety. Whatever is causing his chilling discomfort, Michael seeks a blissful escape from a world spinning out of his control, and entry into a world of fantasy and fun, a world populated by people whose only job is to make you smile, people who live in the world of *Willy Wonka and the Chocolate Factory*, people like the Three Stooges, Abbott and Costello, Buster Keaton, Charlie Chaplin, and, as always, the enchanting Shirley Temple, who, at age six, continues to lure Michael onto the Good Ship Lollipop with the promise that he will, at long last, rest comfortably and dream his troubles away.

23

Breaking News

Back in the late summer of 2007, when Michael and his children moved to the suburbs of northern New Jersey and stayed at the home of the Cascios, the artist's close friends for over two decades, he was genuinely attempting to connect with a loving and normal family. Normality, a long-held dream of Michael's, would never be achieved, but he nonetheless loved being close to people who seemed to be living drama-free lives. During this last visit with the Cascios, he wrote a group of songs — some with Eddie Cascio, son of paterfamilias Dominic — that included "Breaking News." In the tradition of the previously released "Leave Me Alone," "Why You Wanna Trip on Me," "Scream," and "Tabloid Junkie," the composition is a furious lamentation about the abuse that Michael suffers at the hands of the press. This protest is the most personal of all. For the first time in his great body of work, Michael repeatedly calls out his own name in a song.

He decries how everyone wants a piece of Michael

Jackson. The media won't stop stalking Michael Jackson. The world is following every story about Michael Jackson. People want to see him destroyed just because he's Michael Jackson. And then, in the most chilling image of all, Michael Jackson foresees a reporter who cannot wait to write the obituary of Michael Jackson.

That was 2007. This is Sunday, June 21, 2009.

Michael Jackson is home at the Carolwood estate, where he is experiencing great discomfort of body and mind. Emails are flying back and forth between his manager, his promoter, his director, and his doctor. Emergency meetings have been held about the state of Michael's health. Kenny Ortega is convinced that Michael is too weak to rehearse. Frank Dileo is expressing alarm about Michael's aberrant behavior. AEG is disturbed about Michael's use of drugs. Attempting to wean his patient off a nightly dose of propofol, Conrad Murray is telling everyone that, as Michael's primary physician, he has everything under control. According to Murray, whose precarious financial health is dependent on keeping this job and getting Michael through the London concerts, there's no cause for concern. He barks back at Ortega, accusing him of being an "amateur doctor and psychologist." Murray instructs everyone to let him handle the health of Michael, who, he insists, is "physically and emotionally fine."

Meanwhile, Michael feels frozen. Even seated in front of a roaring fireplace, he complains that the cold in his bones will not abate. At one point, a member of his staff calls Cherilyn Lee, the registered nurse Michael found so sympathetic, in spite of her unwillingness to administer propofol. He instructs his staff member to tell her that one side of his body is ice-cold and the other side burning hot. "I knew that somebody had given him something that hit that central nervous system," Lee would later say. She urges the staff member to bring Michael to a hospital, but Michael ignores the advice.

By the end of the weekend, the key players are convinced that this series of fifty super-extravagant shows is on the brink of disintegration. Without a vital, coherent, and committed Michael, the colossal enterprise is about to crash and burn. Hope is fading fast.

Hope seems even dimmer when, against all protestations, Michael goes back for more treatment and Demerol at the office of Dr. Arnold Klein on Monday, June 22, the first day that rehearsals switch from the Forum, in Inglewood, to the Staples Center, in downtown Los Angeles. For those close to Michael, his insistence on visiting Klein is another indication that he'll continue to blow off the rehearsals.

The surrounding pessimism is profound. If Michael doesn't show up tonight, what's the use? The mood of the musicians, backup singers, and dancers is dark. The enormous crew is on edge. The missing Michael has been the source of pervasive anxiety.

And then, unexpectedly, there's breaking news: Michael reemerges. His presence is nothing short of magical, his impassioned participation in the rehearsals incandescent. He is energized; he is inspired. Michael's sudden and urgent recommitment renews everyone's spirits, turning the mood from morose to jubilant.

His life force is infectious as he runs through full-dress rehearsals with studied deliberation. His singing is subtle, lyrical, finely tuned to the subjects at hand. His dancing has returned to form—fluid, easy, relaxed—as he effortlessly glides above and below the rhythms of his sensuous songs. Body and soul are intact. His confidence is back. His grace is back. The singular elegance has never been more evident in this supremely self-assured performer.

As he works with his musicians—especially keyboardist Michael Bearden, drummer Jonathan "Sugarfoot" Moffett, guitarists Tommy Organ and Orianthi Panagaris, percussionist Bashiri Johnson, and bassist Alex Al—his nuanced critiques are especially illuminating. On "The Way You Make Me Feel," for instance, he elongates an already intoxicating groove. "You gotta let it simmer," he tells his band. "Let it just bathe in the moonlight."

After the first night of what everyone considers a brilliant rehearsal, Michael is understandably excited. He's even jovial. His creative juices are flowing. He renews work on a song about the environment that he calls "Breathe." He phones his dear friend Deepak Chopra for help with the lyrics, saying in a voice message that "I've got some really good news to share with you." In a cruel twist of irony, "Breathe" will be the last song Michael will ever write.

As usual, all this stimulation impedes his sleep. Michael

looks for his usual IV drip of propofol. But according to Dr. Conrad Murray, who wants to free his patient of a chronic dependency on the drug, he administers a smaller dose of propofol augmented by two benzodiazepines — lorazepam and Versed — to calm Michael's mind and eventually bring on sleep.

♪ ♪ ♪

The artists, crew members, and executives gathered at the Staples Center the following night, on Tuesday, June 23, wonder whether Michael will show up or revert to another disappearing act.

When he shows, the joy is palpable. Once again, he's ready to work, ready to run through the sequence of songs, each of which incorporates complex choreography that no one who has missed as many rehearsals as Michael could possibly perform. Defying reason, Michael negotiates each routine with consummate mastery. As he rehearses the duet "I Just Can't Stop Loving You" with singer Judith Hill, his voice is radiant, his gesticulations a study in grace.

Tohme Tohme, who has come to the Staples Center to watch the rehearsals, is given an all-access pass by AEG's Randy Phillips and referred to as "Michael's manager" — this in spite of the fact that he has not really seen Michael in over a month. When Tohme Tohme does see Michael during a break, the men embrace warmly. And because Michael, like his mentor, Berry Gordy, delights in sparking competition among his staff, he says to Frank Dileo, who is standing close by, "Come here and give your boss a hug." Dileo ignores the request. Once again, the question is back on the table: who's managing Michael?

But the question hardly seems to matter in the face of Michael's fresh devotion to the This Is It shows. Even when, to prudently preserve his strength, he is not singing at full voice, his elocution and phrasing are vintage Michael. Even when, for the same reason, his dance steps are suggestive rather than fully realized, he nonetheless moves with sublime poise and self-assurance.

Tuesday night is another successful rehearsal. Whether his main man is Tohme Tohme or Frank Dileo or Mickey Mouse, no one seems to care. Michael has shown up for a second consecutive night. Michael is back. Michael is in rare form. Michael is committed to more than a good show in London: he's fiercely determined to put on a *great* show— a record-breaking, mind-boggling, jaw-dropping show.

Michael the miraculous performer has found new life, new energy, new motivation, that is felt by everyone in the cavernous Staples Center. The frightening condition that made his body feel hot and cold at the same time has, at least for now, subsided. He understands the sudden change in his physical and emotional condition as a lifelong reaction—a spectacularly positive reaction—to the challenge of performing. Ever since he was a kid, he has been conditioned to meet that challenge. That is the lesson he absorbed during his formative years, taught first by his father and then by Berry Gordy—two harsh taskmasters, two men who demanded perfection while insisting that, no matter the circumstances, an artist must rise to the occasion, step onstage, and slay the audience.

Michael is grateful to be back in that mind-set. The closer to showtime, the more energy he generates.

Now it's time to go home and rest up so he can hit the stage again tomorrow night. That's possible as long as the artist can get a good night's sleep.

When he arrives at the Carolwood estate, Dr. Murray wants Michael to take only two medicines—lorazepam and Versed—and forgo the propofol entirely. Michael is reluctant. He has been stimulated by the successful rehearsal and is convinced that only propofol will do the job. He agrees, however, to try Murray's plan. To his surprise, the plan works. For the first time in months, Michael is able to fall asleep without the aid of the substance he calls milk, the drug that, according to medical protocol, should be administered only by an anesthesiologist in a closely monitored hospital setting.

Michael wakes up the next day reasonably refreshed.

Things are looking up.

He looks forward to tonight's rehearsal with renewed hope.

His children are happy, he is happy, and there is every reason to believe that he has at long last reclaimed that elusive groove—not merely the rhythmic groove, but the big groove, the cosmic groove, the groove that keeps him moving past all obstacles, the groove that makes his life livable and his art phenomenal.

213

24

"Give Me Your All — Your Endurance, Your Patience, Your Understanding"

Wednesday, June 24, 2009

If the two previous rehearsals were seen as great successes, this one is spectacular.

Kenny Ortega calls Michael's performance "bioluminescent."

Randy Phillips calls it "fantastic."

In Michael's mind, he is merely doing what he has done his entire life: demonstrate his extraordinary professionalism. His work ethic is more than "the show must go on." As an entertainer, he is not satisfied until he drains himself of every last bit of creative energy.

Before this week began, many doubted whether that entertainer would ever reemerge. But on Monday night,

Michael dispelled those doubts. On Tuesday, the doubters were believers, and now, on Wednesday, the believers — the singers, dancers, promoters, managers, lighting directors, choreographers, wardrobe staff, crew hands — have become celebrants, openly cheering Michael's every move.

Without being told what Michael has endured these past sixteen weeks since the announcement of the This Is It shows in London, those involved with the rehearsals have sensed his enormous struggle. They have seen him down and withdrawn; they have understood that his absence has resulted from a deep and enigmatic depression of spirit. And now that he has returned, now that the dark clouds have parted, these people bathe in the light of his victory. He has beat back the demons that have kept him from fully engaging in the work he was born to do. In Michael's mind, that work transcends entertainment. He must reascend to the pop culture pulpit of preaching.

A cherry picker becomes his pulpit. As he steps on the hydraulic crane that rises off the stage and moves high over the arena, he sings his "Earth Song," the heart of This Is It's moral message. The song is sung before a back-screen sequence of lush nature imagery, building to a crescendo in the Amazon rain forest, where a small girl stands up to the onslaught of a massive bulldozer. For several long and thrilling minutes, Michael is literally above it all. Singing of the planet's despair, he works through his own despair. His moans, cries, and laments force us to face our own culpability. His personal witness to environmental destruction is devastating. As the crane swings from one side of the arena to another—now higher, now lower—Michael preaches with fiery conviction. His questions reverberate in every corner of the empty hall. In an anguished voice he sings out the impassioned questions: What about man's selfish neglect? What about the unexplained indifference of God? There are no answers, only questions followed by questions: What about dying children? What about death itself? And, over and over again, what about us? What is our part in this decaying process? And can we—can he—ever change?

If "Earth Song" is Michael's most searing sociopolitical statement, "Billie Jean" is his most personal. His dancers, awed by the power of his performance, stand in front of the stage and wildly cheer him on as he breaks into the boldest and baddest of all his grooves. Watching him, we, like his dancers, get the feeling that he has forgotten this is a rehearsal. He is on another plateau altogether, a transcendent place once described by poet W. B. Yeats: "O body swayed to music, O brightening glance, / How can we know the dancer from the dance?" Michael becomes the living answer to that unanswerable question. He simply *is*. He *is* the song; he *is* the dance; he *is* the unsolved mystery that sits at the dark center of his story; he *is*, at the same time, both the story and the storyteller. His drama, his funk, his sexuality, his anger, his passion, all find form in this single song that he is performing at this very moment, in front of a handful of colleagues, most of them half his age, who look up to him like acolytes looking up to a dancing, singing saint.

For the duration of the long rehearsal, Michael continues to lose himself — or find himself — in every song and every dance. The singing and dancing become a single organic act, a perfect marriage of motion leading voice and voice leading motion. He approaches each category of composition with the empathy of a great actor: he plays the gothic "Thriller" with terrifying intensity; he plays the hounded superstar in "Dirty Diana" with frightening vulnerability. As the "Smooth Criminal," he slouches with Astaire-like aloofness. As the provocateur in "Wanna Be Startin' Somethin'," he prances with playful swagger. As the oppressed in "They Don't Care About Us," he marches with lethal defiance.

So, yes, there is reason for rejoicing. And even though, as is his customary practice, Michael is holding back to conserve his voice — he has a touch of laryngitis — for the actual performances, he still gives enough of himself to excite his colleagues and show them that they are part of something stupendous.

In going through the show, Michael is far from perfect. He leans heavily on Kenny Ortega to refamiliarize him with the intricate staging. But there is never a hint of hesitation or self-doubt about his ability to command this mammoth operation. He is thoughtful and precise about giving directions concerning cues, lighting, and pacing. He knows exactly what is needed to maximize the drama.

In his eyes, those around him recognize his drive and determination. They clearly see that when he hits the London stage, he will be off the wall. He will be dangerous. He will be bad. He will be making history. He will be the man in the mirror. He will be shedding his blood on the dance floor. He will be invincible. He will be every character — every emotion and every attitude — that he has ever assumed. He will become his art, and his art will be radiant.

It's past midnight when Michael leaves the Staples Center, but before he does, he, his dancers and singers and musicians, and director Kenny Ortega form a circle in which Michael addresses the group.

"Everyone is doing a great job, and just continue to believe and have faith," he says. "Give me your all — your endurance, your patience, your understanding... It's an adventure, it's a great adventure, and it's nothing to be nervous about.

"They just want wonderful experiences. They want escapism. We want to take them to places they have never been before. We want to show them talent they have never seen before. So give your all.

"I love you all. We're a family. Just know that we're a family. We're bringing love back into the world to remind the world that love is important... We're all one. To care for the planet, we only have four years to get it right — or for us it's irreversible damage we've done. So I have an important message to give.

"I thank you for your cooperation... Thank you... A big thank-you."

With that, he follows his entourage outside the arena.

Randy Phillips walks with him. At one point Michael turns to the AEG chief and says, "Thank you for getting me here. I got it now. I know I can do this. I'll take it from here."

He'll be back tomorrow for another spirited rehearsal.

All he needs now is a good night's rest.

25

June 25, 2009

Michael didn't write "Man in the Mirror"—Siedah Garrett and Glen Ballard did—but he relates to the lyrics as though they sprang from his very soul. He sees himself walking out into the cold, turning up his collar as the freezing wind reveals the reality of starving children and homeless people the world over. He knows that he has been, as the song says, the victim of a selfish love. He knows that he has been obsessively self-absorbed. And he knows that this isn't who he wants to be. He wants to be released from the prison of his own ego. He wants to devote himself to helping others—the scarred widow; the brokenhearted, defeated by washed-out dreams. His dream is to transcend himself and his endless concerns—*Will my show be the greatest? Will my music set new sales records? Will my iconography be cleansed of all blemishes?*—and concentrate on the issues that matter: the welfare of others, the welfare of the planet.

Over the decades, Michael has looked at the man in the

mirror and not liked what he has seen. For a thousand different reasons, his appearance has been unacceptable, even repulsive, to his own eyes. He has used his vast resources to change that appearance, but in doing so, he has been caught up in a hopeless dilemma. The changes have not brought him happiness. The changes have not calmed his restless soul. The perfection he has sought in himself — in both his physical body and the body of his artistic work — is an illusion. The real change, he finally understands, will happen when he moves beyond himself. On the deepest level, that's what it means to ask himself — to demand of himself — that he change his ways. The metaphor of the mirror couldn't be any clearer. Michael remembers the myth of Narcissus, who was fixated by the beauty of his own image in a pool of water. Because he didn't understand the phenomenon of a mirrorlike reflection, his self-fixation caused him to drown.

The man in the mirror does not want to drown in self-obsession. The man in the mirror does not want to die. He wants to live; he wants to raise his children to be strong and caring human beings. He wants to be a strong and caring human being. And he is. After a lifetime of battling an army of demons of every stripe, he is once again ready to declare victory. "Man in the Mirror," the song that will conclude his London shows, will also open a new chapter in his life.

Optimism is a beautiful thing, Michael reflects after returning to the Carolwood estate. Optimism is rooted in hope, and hope is rooted in faith. Michael's faith is strong. He has seen drive and desire return to his heart like long lost friends. He has felt the powerful camaraderie of his colleagues. He has learned that this project, so fraught with overwhelming problems, is suddenly not a problem at all. It's in him to do this; it always has been. He finally envisions this long series of concerts with clarity.

The vision excites his mind, and his mind moves into overdrive. He goes over all the songs that he has rehearsed. He makes mental notes about how to refine a gesture here and a dance move there. He can't stop reviewing and thinking and relishing the happiness coursing through his spirit.

All this means that he can't sleep.

Because Murray wants to keep Michael on a non-propofol program, at 1:30 a.m. the doctor gives him ten milligrams of Valium.

But Michael's overstimulated mind is stronger than the Valium, and at 2 a.m. he is still awake. Using an IV drip, Murray injects him with two milligrams of another drug often used for anxiety: Ativan.

The Ativan doesn't work.

It's 3 a.m. Michael's excited optimism is turning into anxiety about his inability to sleep. If he's to realize another great rehearsal tomorrow — and he's determined to do just that — he can't afford to be up all night.

Still unwilling to go to the propofol, Murray injects Michael with two milligrams of the benzodiazepine drug Versed, another heavy sedative.

Tossing and turning, Michael grows frantic. He wants sleep. He needs sleep. He cannot tolerate this state of insomnia when all the good feelings are turning bad. His mind is filling with fear. His mind is too active. His mind goes back to the words of Hamlet: "By a sleep to say we end / The heartache and the thousand natural shocks / That flesh is heir to: 'tis a consummation / Devoutly to be . wished." He wants to end the heartache of this free-floating anxiety; he wants to stop the thousand natural shocks; he wants the consummation brought by sweet unconsciousness. He thinks of the words of Henry IV, who cries, "O sleep, O gentle sleep, / Nature's soft nurse, how have I frighted thee, / That thou no more wilt weigh my eyelids down / And steep my senses in forgetfulness?" Michael wants to forget the agony of sleeplessness. He wants to be comforted by nature's soft nurse. He wants to sleep.

Dark night turns light. At dawn Michael is wide-awake. At 5 a.m. Murray gives him two more milligrams of Ativan, but the Ativan has no effect. Michael wants the one substance he knows will work. He wants his milk.

But Murray, convinced that this strong combination of drugs will eventually prove effective, still refuses.

The clock keeps ticking.

Michael's anxiety keeps building.

Now it is 6 a.m., the bright sunshine blocked by the curtains.

Now it is six thirty.

Michael is still awake. Michael is more miserable than ever.

Now it is seven thirty.

Murray reaches for the Versed and injects Michael with another two milligrams. This has to work.

224

It doesn't.

Eight a.m. Nine a.m.

Michael still cannot sleep, cannot abide the anxiety.

Ten a.m.

Michael is frantic.

Ten forty a.m.

Michael has been up all night, all morning. Michael is insisting that Murray abandon his fruitless plan and give him what he needs. It is as though he is re-creating the drama in the song "Morphine": "Today he wants it twice as bad...Yesterday you had his trust / Today he's taking twice as much."

Murray capitulates.

Using the IV drip, he pushes twenty-five milligrams of propofol into Michael's veins.

At long last, the great artist finally goes under.

Little more than a half hour later, Murray is distracted. He makes three phone calls. The first is to his office in Las Vegas; it lasts thirty-one minutes. The second call, a short one, is to a patient. The third call is to a cocktail waitress in Houston. It is during the third call—shortly before noon—that the physician finally realizes that something is terribly wrong. Michael has stopped breathing. The doctor drops the receiver and runs to Michael's side, where he frantically begins performing CPR.

It is too late. Michael has fallen into a full cardiac arrest.

At twenty-one minutes past noon, 911 is called.

At twenty-six minutes past noon, paramedics arrive.

At fifty-seven minutes past noon, paramedics pronounce Michael dead.

He is taken in an ambulance to the nearby UCLA Medical Center, where all further attempts to revive him prove futile.

Experts will later speculate that in a hospital setting—with a heart monitor, blood pressure monitor, and defibrillator, none of which were present at Carolwood—his life could have been saved.

The official time of death is given as 2:26 p.m.

It is a little after midnight in London when fans, counting down the days before Michael's opening show at the O$_2$, begin hearing reports. Texts and emails furiously fly over the city. Social media blows up. And everywhere the reaction is incredulity. It must be a hoax.

In Tokyo it is already Friday morning. Tens of millions of people awaken to the news. Searching for the truth, hoping against hope that it is merely a ruse, anxiety-ridden Michael fans crash website after website, typing in their queries and requests: "Is Michael dead?" "Tell me this is some sick joke." "Affirm that Michael is alive."

Johannesburg, Moscow, São Paulo, Bayreuth, Berlin, Lisbon, Istanbul. Continent by continent, country by country, city by city, village by village, the news sinks in. The tragic truth can no longer be denied.

On that same Thursday, the day of his death, I am traveling to where my journey — as well as Michael's — began. I am in our home state of Indiana, where I've been invited to address a body of educators in Indianapolis. As I'm walking from the car to the auditorium, my cell phone goes ballistic with a series of messages, all saying the same thing: Michael Jackson is dead at fifty. I stagger to the podium. I have no choice but to tell the assemblage, "It pains me beyond measure to bring this news. But I can't even think about beginning my lecture today without acknowledging the loss of our most beloved native son." When I announce the death of Michael, there are gasps and cries. Grown men and women openly weep. I weep.

When the weeping is over, I have no choice but to deliver my talk. I manage to get through the ordeal, but I'm not all right. I'm not all there. I can't stop thinking of Michael. And neither can the rest of the world.

26

Before You Judge Me

The ensuing drama brought on by Michael's demise mirrored the preceding drama of his life on earth.

The autopsy report gave the cause of death as "acute propofol intoxication" and indicated that, surprisingly, in most respects Michael was in good health. The report stated further, "Full patient monitoring is required anytime propofol is given. The most essential monitor is a person trained in anesthesia and in resuscitation who is continuously present and not involved in the ongoing surgical/diagnostic procedure." Dr. David Adams, the anesthesiologist whom Michael and Murray interviewed in Las Vegas but didn't hire, could have been that person.

Two and a half years later, on November 29, 2011, Dr. Conrad Murray was sentenced to four years for involuntary manslaughter. He was released after serving two years in the Men's Central Jail in downtown Los Angeles.

On October 2, 2013, Michael's mother, Katherine Jackson, lost a $1.5 billion negligence lawsuit against AEG, claiming that the promoters were responsible for her son's death.

Amid a storm of controversies, Michael's estate, administered by his onetime attorney John Branca and music executive John McClain, paid off his enormous debts and, through a brilliant recrafting of the Michael Jackson brand, earned millions for Michael's beneficiaries named in his will: his three children and his mother, charged with their care.

♪ ♪ ♪

This book began with a simple query: what happened in the last sixteen weeks of Michael's life that caused his tragically premature death? After scrutinizing the litany of facts and poring over thousands upon thousands of pages — books, articles, and court transcripts — I find myself moving toward a conclusion that inevitably takes the form of still another question.

Given the extraordinary obstacles he faced, the stresses that pulled him apart, how did Michael survive as long as he did? How did he manage to negotiate the pernicious psychological and cultural conundrums he faced as a hypersensitive child, vulnerable teenager, and wildly conflicted adult?

In other words, what gave Michael the fortitude to prevail for over four decades as an artist of international stature and influence?

To answer the question, I accept Michael's admonition when, in his song "Childhood," he wrote, "Before you judge me, try hard to love me."

Loving Michael means understanding Michael. And understanding Michael means opening our hearts to both the luminous beauty and frightful pain inherent in his life story. All we can do is go back and attempt to answer the most haunting and essential question of all:

Who, exactly, is Michael Jackson?

Michael is six and he is thinking that the ability to sing is the greatest gift God has ever given him. He can't understand this gift as anything other than a divine present. Only months before, his mother pointed out to his father that Michael can sing, and he has recently joined the family band. Now, though, he is going to sing a solo in front of the elementary school where he attends first grade. He chooses "Climb Ev'ry Mountain" because it is his favorite song from a film he has recently seen, *The Sound of Music.* He is too young to describe the emotions flooding his heart, too young to use the word "inspiring." But he is clearly inspired. In his simple white shirt and black trousers, he faces the students and teachers with uncanny confidence. The confidence does not come from any prior experience. It does not come from arrogance. Young Michael radiates confidence because of his belief that he has been chosen as the right messenger — even the righteous messenger — to tell this story of hope. His voice never wavers, his pitch never falters. The pure beauty of his voice leaves his audience stunned. When he has sung

231

the last perfect note, the onlookers rise to their feet and shout their approval. At this moment, he realizes his life's calling. He has never felt more alive.

He has never felt more alive, more excited, than when he arrives in Los Angeles at the end of the sixties and finds himself shuttling back and forth between the luxurious homes of Berry Gordy and Diana Ross. In the privileged seclusion of Beverly Hills, there is no harsh winter, no visible poverty. Given the sensational string of number one Jackson 5 hits, there seems to be no limit to the group's potential. In a matter of months, Michael's world has turned from gray to golden. For the first time, he is reading books about the great artists who express the beauty of human life in highly personal ways. He cannot help but wonder if he himself can grow into such an artist. The question seems to be answered when Michael, just barely a teenager, has his first solo hit, "Got to Be There." A deep equivocation emerges: his devotion to his family on one hand, his passion for self-expression on the other.

He has never felt more alive, more curious, than when, seeking creative freedom, he and his brothers leave the brilliant Motown producers and writers, whom he has studied for years, and sign with CBS/Epic records, where they are teamed with the equally brilliant writer-producers

Gamble and Huff. Michael's concentration intensifies. His creative courage is galvanized as he realizes his own ability to craft a sound all his own. The studio becomes his dojo, and before the age of twenty, he becomes a young master.

Excitement is in the air, and Michael has never felt more alive than when he finds himself on a spectacular movie set at Astoria Studios in Queens, New York, where, costumed as the Scarecrow, hungry for knowledge—a theatrical metaphor close to his heart—he becomes the breakout star in *The Wiz*. Excitement gains even more momentum when, in reading the film's script, he recognizes that spiritual teaching can come from outside the narrow confines of his childhood church. From his costar Diana Ross and the film's screenwriter, Joel Schumacher, Michael learns about the teachings of Werner Erhard and the est movement, which stresses self-reliance, self-assertion, and self-belief.

The Scarecrow does, in fact, locate his intelligence. His intelligence has always been a part of him; it simply required recognition. The Wiz, as played by Richard Pryor, may be a false guru, but Quincy Jones, the musical force behind the film, is real. His cultural knowledge is vast. Michael taps him as his next great teacher, and together they dance into the disco era with a seamless, sensuous sound that will put Michael's career on a trajectory that sets the pop music world aflame.

Excitedly, thrillingly, Michael tells us to get on the floor and "dance with me." We accept. We dance. We follow his every fabulous move.

Michael is excited, even thrilled, to finally separate himself from a tyrannical father, dependent brothers, and a church whose doctrines he no longer believes. He is nearly thirty when, rich beyond reason, he finally finds the strength to leave his parents' house and create a home entirely his own. For Michael, home is a fairy tale. Home is an amusement park. Home is a hideaway. Home is a child's playhouse. Home is a comforting dream, a place where he can act the fool and engage in silly pranks. Home is where he welcomes whomever he likes, anyone and everyone who excites his imagination and rewards him with warm feelings of acceptance. Aging movie stars. Children. Gurus. Families that act as surrogates for his own warring family.

Michael is exhilarated when he realizes that, after working for a decade with master musician Quincy Jones, his own musical powers have never been stronger, his own musical vision never more focused. He will surpass the seemingly unsurpassable. He will go beyond the scope of *Off the Wall*, *Thriller*, and *Bad*. He will find daring new collaborators and create daring new work. He will move from the incandescent *Dangerous* to the even more ambitious *HIStory*. He will join and unjoin the genres in a way that no one has ever done before. He will push the boundaries of musical film. He will don fat suits and play the part of his sworn enemies, wooing and winning his public with the sheer dazzle of his dance. Creatively, he will no longer require the support of a strongman—a Joseph, a Berry, or a Quincy. He will be out there alone, on his own, and he will continue to create.

His spirit is soaring when he is assured that the vicious attacks against him—attacks emanating from avaricious predators looking to extort him for millions, attacks accusing him of being perversely abnormal—will finally be silenced when he does what he has long sought to do: create a normal family of his own. His determination will defeat all barriers, all skeptics. When one wife proves incompatible, he will try again. When a second wife is equally incompatible, his drive is not diminished. On his own enigmatic terms, he succeeds. His focus is not on a spouse; it is on progeny, his own beloved brood of children who will finally assuage the terrible loneliness that has haunted him since childhood, children who will be raised to respect the values he himself so deeply respects: love, tolerance, and compassion.

His excitement has reached new heights. With all his heart he is feeling that this is a man he can trust, a documentarian whose empathetic portrayal of Princess Diana turned world opinion in her favor. The princess was suddenly viewed with great sympathy. After years of being brutalized by the press, Michael yearns for the same sympathy, the same turnaround in his favor. For eight months he allows British filmmaker Martin Bashir full access. Michael's advisors warn him that such openness is ill-advised and even potentially dangerous. Michael doesn't agree. It is 2003. A decade has passed since the accusation that led to a torrent of negative press whose impact, in Michael's mind, has permanently altered the world's perception of him. For all the right reasons, he wants that perception changed. He wants to be seen, understood, and loved for who he is. Michael knows that his openhearted approach, his trust in a documentarian who unabashedly expresses his admiration for him, will result in a much-needed makeover of his image.

The television film, *Living with Michael Jackson*, becomes a scandal. The filmmaker portrays Michael in the worst possible light. Remarks are pulled out of context, and Michael's behavior is made to seem suspect, if not criminal. Soon after, criminal charges are filed and Michael is forced to stand trial for sixteen weeks, during which the evidence against him falls apart. He is acquitted on every count.

At trial's end, Michael collapses. He leaves the Western world behind. There is speculation that this ordeal, the most painful of his life, will destroy his spirit and forever dampen his creative fire.

The fire is back, the spirit is renewed, and in the few days just before his death, Michael has never felt more alive.

Michael is thinking. Michael is feeling. In his mind, in his heart, in the deepest part of his soul, the dragons have been slayed. The poisonous doubts have been purged. His identification as an artist and the power and purity of his art have overcome the negative forces.

He is thinking of everything that has transpired since he announced the This Is It shows in London sixteen weeks earlier — the same number of weeks it took to endure his 2005 trial, after which he emerged victorious. Now he's certain that he will emerge victorious again.

After three brilliant rehearsals, Michael is back in the groove. While the revolving door of advisors, managers, and promoters may have made him dizzy at first, he has now finally found stability.

He is excited that a good portion of his extraordinary body of work will once again be on display for the world to see. There are the beloved songs, the bewitching dances, the ingenious short films. There's the full range of every emotion in his head and heart — anger and frustration, joy and doubt — as well as his social concerns and psychological preoccupations. Plus monsters and gangsters, happiness and hope, the vision of a decaying world, the vision of a healing world, the whole spectrum of life as it has lived inside Michael's mind since he was a little boy.

The show will be spectacular.

The show will be followed by other shows, other songs and dances and movies. The classical music he will compose, the feature films he will create and star in, the pop-rock-soul albums he will release — new, fresh ideas are blossoming at a remarkably rapid rate. He perceives the world as beautiful. The world is wondrous. The world is abundant. The world is filled with endless creative possibilities.

Michael is more alive than ever.

Afterword

My connection to Michael is both personal and passionate.

It began in 1969, the year I turned five. Reared in a Pentecostal household where pop music entertainment was prohibited, I was an obedient child. But when I heard the Jackson 5's initial run of hits, I flipped. And when I learned that, like me, the boys hailed from Indiana, I did a double flip. I crossed the line and became a lifetime fan of a sound that, although secular, struck me with sacred intensity. Michael Jackson was singing the truth.

I completely identified with Michael. His irrepressible energy brought joy to my childhood. Later, I learned that, also like me, he faced the confusion and pain of being raised in a household where religious orthodoxy was accompanied by corporal punishment. We had suffered in similar ways.

Yet Michael's voice was all about happiness and hope. That happiness and hope were illuminated — and wonderfully illustrated — when, in 1971, the Jackson 5 was turned into a Saturday morning cartoon show. I couldn't stop myself from sneaking to watch the program in our family room. I got caught a few times by my parents and paid the price. Despite the punishment, I continued to view Michael's whimsical adventures, in which he always managed to sidestep trouble and emerge victorious, as signposts for freedom. It would be a lifetime later when I could articulate what I was absorbing: an aspirational energy that captured my heart and had me believing in a big wide world outside the confines of the trailer park in which I was raised.

Because I was initially uncomfortable with the strange name Tavis, I secretly renamed myself Michael. I wanted to connect to the same muse that connected Michael to a fountainhead of endless creativity. Michael was almost fourteen when he released his solo album *Ben*, featuring a love song to a rodent. I was nine when I heard it, becoming convinced that, in the anthropomorphically idealized universe of Michael Jackson, even rats are benign creatures worthy of love. Michael comforted me.

Michael excited me as I closely followed his career through the dazzling days of his Gamble and Huff–produced records to his astounding postdisco *Off the Wall* work with Quincy Jones and, of course, the sublimely brilliant *Thriller*. As his mythos broadened, so did my interest in who he was and what he represented. No matter the bizarre nature of his physical transformations or the accusations of his misbehavior, I never stopped admiring his astounding artistry. I never stopped seeking to understand him. I never stopped loving him, as both a brother and a man desperately seeking peace of mind in a show business world ruled by hysteria and hype.

On March 5, 2009, when I heard Michael announce his plan for a series of concerts at London's O$_2$ Arena, I immediately called Miss Katherine, his mother. She has been a devoted fan of my television shows for many years and a person with whom I've always enjoyed a warm rapport.

"I've never asked for a favor before," I said, "and wouldn't be doing it now if the matter wasn't so urgent. I just have to see Michael perform in London this coming summer. I'm happy to pay, but, given the inevitable rush for seats, I just want to make sure I can get in."

"Of course you can, Tavis. I'll make certain that you get a good seat."

With that assurance, I bought my plane ticket, made hotel reservations, and looked forward to July in London.

Then came June 25.

In preparing this text, I had to try to understand the essential character of Michael Jackson—who he was, what he became, and who he wanted to be. I had to paint an authentic portrait of not only his genius as an artist but his colossal contradictions as a man. I had to get inside Michael's head.

I faced the same challenge two years ago, when I wrote *Death of a King*, a novelistic narrative of the last year in the life of Martin Luther King Jr. I stress the word "novelistic." In telling King's story, I wanted to imbue the text with all the excitement and fast-paced rhythm of a novel.

I also wanted to be deeply informed. To achieve this with Michael, I scrutinized a massive amount of material: the transcripts of both the People versus Conrad Murray and Jackson versus AEG, plus scores of biographies, autobiographies, interviews, and essays.

My conjecture about the inner workings of Michael's mind is neither whimsical nor arbitrary. It is a studied reading based on a great many sources. In the final analysis, though, it is an interpretation born out of my own understanding. I view my definition of Jackson's character not as *the* truth, but rather *a* truth, which is to say *my* truth.

The truth about Michael Jackson is elusive and perplexing. He is an artist of enduring complexity. His character assumes mythic proportions—dazzling and often confusing myths perpetuated by both the media and Michael himself. Because he was one of the most documented musicians of the modern age, there is a wealth of material to scrutinize. To help me mold that material into a manageable story, I was, for the fourth time, delighted to be working with David Ritz. On our three previous projects—my own autobiography, *What I Know for Sure*; *Death of a King*; and *My Journey with Maya*—David was an invaluable partner. But on this Michael Jackson project, his role became even more critical. David has made a lifetime study of African American music. For the past forty years, he has worked hand in hand with Ray Charles, Marvin Gaye, Aretha Franklin, B.B. King, Buddy Guy, Etta James, Smokey Robinson, the Neville Brothers, Rick James, Grandmaster Flash, R. Kelly,

Bettye LaVette, and Janet Jackson on their life stories. It is David's conversations with, among others, Janet Jackson, Bobby Taylor, Walter Yetnikoff, Bob Jones, and Marvin Gaye that help give this story such weight. David knows this territory as well as anyone. Beyond relying on his knowledge of and sensitivity to the music, I leaned heavily on his storytelling skills to forge a novel-like narrative fueled by the questions that have haunted me since that sad summer day in 2009.

I too am the beneficiary of a series of long conversations about Michael, in my case with Berry Gordy, Quincy Jones, and Katherine Jackson. I cherish the memory of honoring Mrs. Jackson's request to escort her and her grandchildren Prince, Paris, and Blanket on a private tour of "America I Am: The African American Imprint," a historical and cultural exhibition I curated in October of 2009, just months after Michael's passing. Michael was prominently featured in three separate galleries. All three times that Mrs. Jackson faced her son's image, she broke down in tears. In those moments I realized that, no matter how deeply we love Michael, there will always be a distance between us and him. Not so for Mrs. Jackson. He was, and will always remain, her baby.

It is my hope that this text will shed light on Michael's creative life. I view my study of his artistic genius as a way to enhance my own work and witness.

Michael Jackson is forever. Family, fans, friends, and

writers will forever seek to reconnect with him. If nothing else, I offer this book as a way to not only reconnect but make sense of those tremendously powerful forces that both inspired his soaring art and contributed to his tragic demise.

Acknowledgments

From Tavis Smiley:

To God the Creator, and to Katherine and Joseph Jackson for the gift of their son Michael.

Some of us is not the sum of us. Each of us wants our life's work to be judged by the sum total, not some parts. I certainly do.

The sum of Michael Joseph Jackson is to be reckoned with. Now and forever. Thank you, Michael.

And, finally, to all those who helped to produce this detailed account of his monumental contribution, more than adequately told: my collaborator par excellence David Ritz, my more than able researcher Jared Hernandez, agent

David Vigliano, and, lastly, the team at Little, Brown: Reagan Arthur, John Parsley, Malin von Euler-Hogan, Liz Garriga, Betsy Uhrig.

From David Ritz:

To Tavis for the joy of our ongoing collaboration as writers, friends, and brothers in Christ; superb researcher Jared Hernandez, editors John Parsley and Malin von Euler-Hogan, publisher Reagan Arthur, agent David Vigliano, my family—Roberta, Alison, Jessica, Henry, Jim, Charlotte, Alden, Jimmy, Isaac, Elizabeth, and Esther—and my friends Harry Weinger, Herb Powell, Alan Eisenstock, Juan Moscoso, and John Tayloe.

Bibliography

Texts and Primary Sources

Adams, Dr. David. Testimony, *Katherine Jackson v. AEG Live, LLC, et al.*, August 21, 2013.

Alvarez, Nicole. Testimony at the Los Angeles Superior Court, October 4, 2011.

Andersen, Christopher. *Michael Jackson: Unauthorized.* New York: Simon & Schuster, 1994.

Andrews, Bart. *Out of the Madness: The Strictly Unauthorized Biography of Janet Jackson.* London: Headline Book Publishing, 1994.

Autopsy Report: Jackson, Michael Joseph — Case No. 2009 — 04415. County of Los Angeles Department of Coroner.

Bani, Arno. *Michael Jackson: Auction.* New York: Hachette Livre (Acc), 2010.

Bego, Mark. *Michael!* New York: Pinnacle Books, 1984.

Boteach, Rabbi Shmuley. *The Michael Jackson Tapes: A Tragic Icon Reveals His Soul in Intimate Conversation.* New York: Vanguard Press, 2009.

Bush, Michael. *The King of Style: Dressing Michael Jackson.* San Rafael: Insight Editions, 2012.

Cascio, Frank, with Hilary Liftin. *My Friend Michael: An Ordinary Friendship with an Extraordinary Man.* New York: HarperCollins Publishers, 2011.

Chase, Kai. Testimony, *Katherine Jackson v. AEG Live, LLC, et al.*, June 18, 2013.

Complaint. *Raymone K. Bain v. Gary, Williams, Parenti, Watson & Gary, P.L.* In the Superior Court for the District of Columbia, May 3, 2013.

Dimond, Diane. *Be Careful Who You Love: Inside the Michael Jackson Case.* New York: Atria, 2005.

EBONY Magazine. *Ebony Special Tribute: Michael Jackson in His Own Words.* Chicago: Johnson Publishing Company, 2009.

Editors of *Rolling Stone*, The. *Michael.* New York: Rolling Stone, LLC, 2009.

Fast, Susan. *Michael Jackson's Dangerous.* New York: Bloomsbury Academic, 2014.

Geller, Larry. *Leaves of Elvis' Garden: The Song of His Soul.* Beverly Hills: Bell Rock Publishing, 2008.

George, Nelson. *The Michael Jackson Story.* New York: Dell, 1983.

_____. *Thriller: The Musical Life of Michael Jackson.* Boston: De Capo Press, 2010.

_____. *Where Did Our Love Go?: The Rise and Fall of the Motown Sound.* New York: St. Martin's Press, 1985.

Gordy, Berry. *To Be Loved: The Music, the Magic, the Memories of Motown.* New York: Warner Books, 1994.

Greenburg, Zack O'Malley. *Michael Jackson, Inc.: The Rise, Fall, and Rebirth of a Billion-Dollar Empire.* New York: Atria Books, 2014.

Halperin, Ian. *Unmasked: The Final Years of Michael Jackson.* New York: Pocket Books, 2009.

Halstead, Craig, and Chris Cadman. *Michael Jackson: The Solo Years.* Hertford: AuthorsOnLine Ltd., 2003.

Harris, Neil. *Humbug: The Art of P. T. Barnum.* Chicago: University of Chicago Press, 1973.

Jackson, Janet, with David Ritz. *True You: A Journey to Finding and Loving Yourself.* New York: Simon & Schuster, 2011.

Jackson, Jermaine. *You Are Not Alone: Michael: Through a Brother's Eyes.* New York: Touchstone, 2011.

Jackson, Katherine, with Richard Wiseman. *My Family, the Jacksons.* London: St. Martin's Press, 1990.

Jackson, La Toya, with Patricia Romanowski. *La Toya: Growing Up in the Jackson Family.* Post Falls: Century, 1990.

_____, with Jeffré Phillips. *Starting Over.* Beverly Hills: Ja-Tail Publishing Company, 2011.

Jackson, Margaret Maldonado. *Jackson Family Values: Memories of Madness.* Beverly Hills: Dove Books, 1995.

Jackson, Michael. *Dancing the Dream.* New York: Doubleday, 2009.

_____. Letter to Leonard Rowe. Dated March 25, 2009.

_____. Letter to Leonard Rowe. Dated May 20, 2009.

_____. *Moonwalk.* New York: Crown Publishing Group, 2009.

Jackson, Paris-Michael. Deposition. Superior Court of the State of California, March 21, 2013.

Jefferson, Margo. *On Michael Jackson.* New York: Pantheon Books, 2006.

Jones, Bob, with Stacy Brown. *Michael Jackson: The Man Behind the Mask.* New York: SelectBooks, 2005.

Katherine Jackson v. AEG Live, LLC, et al. Trial transcripts, April 2, 2013–October 12, 2013.

King, Jason. *Michael Jackson Treasures: Celebrating the King of Pop in Memorabilia and Photos.* New York: Fall River Press, 2009.

King, Tom. *The Operator: David Geffen Builds, Buys, and Sells the New Hollywood.* New York: Random House, 2000.

Kipling, Rudyard. "If," in *Kipling: Poems.* New York: Knopf, 2007.

Knopper, Steve. *MJ: The Genius of Michael Jackson.* New York: Scribner, 2015.

Lee, Cherilyn. Testimony at the Los Angeles Superior Court, August 28, 2013.

Lopez, Tim. Testimony at the Los Angeles Superior Court, October 4, 2011.

Marsh, Dave. *Trapped: Michael Jackson and the Crossover Dream.* New York: Bantam Books, 1985.

"Michael Jackson Appoints New Management: Leonard Rowe, legendary promoter, to steer singer's latest comeback." Champion Management Press Release, March 26, 2009.

Mottola, Tommy, with Cal Fussman. *Hitmaker: The Man and His Music*. New York: Hachette Book Group, 2013.

Payne, Travis. Testimony at the Los Angeles Superior Court, May 28, 2013.

People of the State of California v. Conrad Robert Murray. Trial transcripts, September 27, 2011–November 11, 2011.

Posner, Gerald. *Motown: Music, Money, Sex, and Power*. New York: Random House, 2002.

Ritz, David, ed. *Elvis by the Presleys*. New York: Crown Archetype, 2005.

Ross, Diana. *Secrets of a Sparrow: Memoirs*. New York: Villard Books, 1993.

Rousseau, Jean-Jacques. *Emile, or On Education*. Ed. Allan Bloom. New York: Basic Books, 1979.

Rowe, Leonard. *What Really Happened to Michael Jackson, the King of Pop*. Suwanee: Linell-Diamond Enterprises, LLC, 2010.

Shakespeare, William. *Hamlet*. Ed. Barbara A. Mowat and Paul Werstine. New York: Simon & Schuster, 1992.

_____. *Henry IV, Part 2*. Ed. Barbara A. Mowat and Paul Werstine. New York: Washington Square Press, 1999.

Shields, Damien. *Xscape Origins: The Songs and Stories Michael Jackson Left Behind*. Akron: Modegy, LLC, 2015.

Sullivan, Randall. *Untouchable: The Strange Life and Tragic Death of Michael Jackson*. New York: Grove Press, 2012.

Taraborrelli, J. Randy. *Michael Jackson: The Magic, the Madness, the Whole Story, 1958–2009*. New York: Grand Central Publishing, 2010.

Transcript. Ed Bradley interviews Michael Jackson. *60 Minutes*. CBS, December 2003.

Transcript. Geraldo Rivera interviews Michael Jackson. *At Large with Geraldo Rivera*. Fox News, May 2, 2005.

Transcript. Jesse Jackson interviews Michael Jackson. *Keep Hope Alive*, March 27, 2005. Radio.

Transcript. Recorded interview of Conrad Murray. Los Angeles Police Department Internal Affairs Group, June 27, 2009.

Vogel, Joseph. *Man in the Music: The Creative Life and Work of Michael Jackson*. New York: Sterling, 2011.

Waldman, Dr. Robert. Testimony at the Los Angeles Superior Court, October 27, 2011.

Watchtower Bible and Tract Society of New York, Inc. Letter concerning Michael Jackson's disassociation with the Jehovah's Witnesses, June 8, 1987.

Weisner, Ron, and Alan Goldsher. *Listen Out Loud: A Life in Music—Managing McCartney, Madonna, and Michael Jackson.* Guilford: Lyons Press, 2014.

Whitfield, Bill, and Javon Beard, with Tanner Colby. *Remember the Time: Protecting Michael Jackson in His Final Days.* New York: Weinstein Books, 2014.

Yeats, W. B. "Among School Children," in *The Collected Poems of W. B. Yeats.* New York: Scribner, 1996.

Yetnikoff, Walter, with David Ritz. *Howling at the Moon.* New York: Broadway Books, 2004.

Newspaper and Magazine Articles

Alexander, Bryan. "The Michael Jackson Case: The Return of the Nanny." *Time*, July 22, 2009.

"Anesthesiologist Testifies Jackson Wanted Him to Go on Tour." *Los Angeles Times*, August 21, 2013.

Baguma, Raymond. "Michael Jackson's Uganda Nanny Comes from Bushenyi." *New Vision*, June 29, 2009.

Brown, Mick. "Elton John Interview." *The Telegraph*, October 25, 2010.

Cannon, Bob. "Michael Jackson's 'Dangerous' Year." *Entertainment Weekly*, December 17, 1993.

Chopra, Deepak. "Remembering Michael." *Time*, June 26, 2009.

Dart, John. "Jackson Out of Jehovah's Witness Sect." *Los Angeles Times*, June 7, 1987.

David, Mark. "Update: Michael 'The White Lady' Jackson." *Variety*, July 5, 2007.

Dillon, Nancy. "Gloves Are Off! 'Thriller' Co-Star Ola Ray Sues Michael Jackson for Royalties." *New York Daily News*, May 5, 2009.

_____. "Michael Jackson Trial: Conrad Murray Mistress Recalls Doctor's Phone Call as King of Pop Was Dying." *New York Daily News*, October 4, 2011.

Dillon, Nancy, and Larry McShane. "Michael Jackson's Mother Katherine Is 'Disappointed' by AEG Live's Not-Liable Verdict but Is 'Doing the Best She Can,' Says Lawyer." *New York Daily News*, October 3, 2013.

Dillon, Nancy, and Stephen Rex Brown. "Michael Jackson Wrongful Death Suit." *New York Daily News*, June 20, 2013.

Dimond, Diane. "Doctor Demerol: Michael Jackson Dermatologist Arnold Klein Under Investigation." *Daily Beast*, December 5, 2011.

Elber, Lynn. "AP Exclusive: Insomniac Jackson Begged for Drug." Associated Press, July 1, 2009.

Gold, Todd. "Dumped by Michael Jackson, Former Manager Frank Dileo Bounces Back as One of Hollywood's *GoodFellas*." *People*, October 22, 1990.

Goldman, Andrew. "The First 'Neverland.'" *Daily Beast*, June 26, 2009.

Goleman, Daniel. "Psychologists Examine Appeal of Michael Jackson." *New York Times*, July 9, 1984.

Harris, Chris. "Michael Jackson Sued by Former Publicist, 'Thriller' Star." *Rolling Stone*, May 7, 2009.

Hicks, Tony. "Shirley Temple Cooked Michael Jackson Dinner." *San Jose Mercury News*, February 14, 2014.

Hoffman, Claire. "The Last Days of Michael Jackson." *Rolling Stone*, August 6, 2009.

Kasindorf, Martin. "Jackson Doctor's Girlfriend Called to Testify." *USA Today*, October 4, 2011.

Kellogg, Carolyn. "Michael Jackson, the Bookworm." *Los Angeles Times*, June 27, 2009.

Lee, Chris, and Harriet Ryan. "Deep Pockets Behind Michael Jackson." *Los Angeles Times*, May 31, 2009.

_____. "Michael Jackson Rehearses Near Burbank Airport." *Los Angeles Times*, May 12, 2009.

Messer, Lesley. "Deepak Chopra: Michael Jackson Had Lupus." *People*, June 27, 2009.

"Michael Jackson Ends Tour, Citing Addiction." *New York Times*, November 14, 1993.

"Michael Jackson Eyed Vegas 'Wonderland.'" *Las Vegas Sun*, August 13, 2009.

"No Charge Is Filed in Alleged Extortion of Michael Jackson." *New York Times*, January 25, 1994.

O'Connor, John J. "Michael Jackson Profile on Cable Shows His Star Quality as a Child." *New York Times*, March 12, 1988.

Pareles, Jon. "How Good Is Jackson's 'Bad'?" *New York Times*, September 3, 1987.

_____. "Michael Jackson at 25: A Musical Phenomenon." *New York Times*, January 14, 1984.

_____. "Michael Jackson in the Electronic Wilderness." *New York Times*, November 24, 1991.

_____. "Michael Jackson Is Angry, Understand?" *New York Times*, June 18, 1995.

_____. "Pop: Michael Jackson's 'Bad,' Follow-Up to a Blockbuster." *New York Times*, August 31, 1987.

_____. "To Regain Glory, the New Michael Imitates the Old." *New York Times*, October 28, 2001.

_____. "Tricky Steps from Boy to Superstar." *New York Times*, June 25, 2009.

"Pepsi Drops Sponsorship of Jackson." *Los Angeles Times*, November 15, 1993.

Powers, Ann. "Just What Does Michael Jackson's Story Add Up To?" *New York Times*, February 21, 1993.

Roberts, Randall. "Michael Jackson's Lawyer, Bob Sanger, Talks to West Coast Sound About the Pop Star, His Life — and His Reading Habits." *LA Weekly*, June 25, 2009.

Robinson, Lisa. "The Boy Who Would Be King." *Vanity Fair*, September 2009.

Rohter, Larry. "Jackson Said to Be Near a Deal That Is as Big as His Hits." *New York Times,* November 21, 1990.

Rothenberg, Randall. "Michael Jackson Gets Thriller of Deal to Stay with Sony." *New York Times,* March 21, 1991.

Ryan, Harriet. "Doubts Surfaced Early on Michael Jackson." *Los Angeles Times,* September 2, 2012.

_____. "Michael Jackson Begged for Propofol, Detective Says in Recapping Conrad Murray's Statement." *Los Angeles Times,* January 11, 2011.

Seal, Mark. "The Doctor Will Sue You Now: The Ugly World of Dr. Arnie Klein, Beverly Hills' King of Botox." *Vanity Fair,* March 2012.

Silverman, Stephen M. "Former Nanny Tells of Michael's Drug Use." *People,* June 27, 2009.

Singh, Amar, and Robert Mendick. "Detoxing Brand Jacko." *London Evening Standard,* March 13, 2009.

Sisario, Ben. "Frank Dileo, Michael Jackson's Manager, Dies at 63." *New York Times,* August 24, 2011.

Stevenson, Richard W. "'Thriller,' Can Michael Jackson Beat It?" *New York Times,* November 10, 1991.

Weinraub, Bernard. "Jackson Being Treated Abroad for Addiction, Lawyer Says." *New York Times,* November 16, 1993.

_____. "The Jackson Family Reunited, Sort Of." *New York Times,* February 21, 1994.

_____. "Michael Jackson's Lawyer and Investigator Quit Jobs." *New York Times,* December 22, 1993.

"Will Michael Jackson's Real Manager Please Stand Up." *Encore: The Weekly Performance Industry Magazine,* April 2, 2009.

Web Sources and Online Articles

99 Spanish Gate Dr., Las Vegas, NV, 89113. Zillow.com (accessed May 5, 2015). http://www.zillow.com/homedetails/99-Spanish-Gate -Dr-Las-Vegas-NV-89113/7147564_zpid/.

Allen, Nick. "Michael Jackson Was Being Trained by Incredible Hulk." Telegraph.co.uk, June 30, 2009. http://www.telegraph.co.uk/culture/music/michael-jackson/5699082/Michael-Jackson-was-being-trained-by-Incredible-Hulk.html.

Bosso, Joe. "Michael Jackson: The 7 Guitarists Who Shaped His Sound." MusicRadar.com, June 25, 2010. http://www.musicradar.com/news/guitars/michael-jackson-the-7-guitarists-who-shaped-his-sound-256844/2.

Brown, Campbell. "Transcript of Cherilyn Lee Interview." CNN.com, June 30, 2009. http://ac360.blogs.cnn.com/2009/06/30/transcript-of-cherilyn-lee-interview/.

Bychawski, Adam. "Michael Jackson 'Angry' at 50 London Shows Being Booked." NME.com, June 2, 2009. http://www.nme.com/news/michael-jackson/45043/photo/2.

Chopra, Deepak. "A Tribute to My Friend, Michael Jackson." Beliefnet .com, June 2009. http://www.beliefnet.com/columnists/intentchopra/2009/06/a-tribute-to-my-friend-michael.html.

Chopra, Gotham. "Remembering My Friend Michael Jackson." Beliefnet.com, June 2010. http://www.beliefnet.com/columnists/intentchopra/2010/06/remembering-my-friend-michael.html.

Concepcion, Mariel. "Exclusive: Michael Jackson Was Working on Two Albums." Billboard.com, July 2, 2009. http://www.billboard.com/articles/news/268221/exclusive-michael-jackson-was-working-on-two-albums.

Dasgupta, Piyali. "Michael Asked About the Valley of Death, Says Deepak Chopra." NDTV.com, January 19, 2012. http://movies.ndtv.com/bollywood/michael-asked-about-the-valley-of-death-says-deepak-chopra-623132.

"David Williams Biography." http://www.allmusic.com/artist/david-williams-mn0000233080/biography.

"David Williams: Guitar God to the Stars." Hollywood Sentinel (accessed March 24, 2015). http://www.thehollywoodsentinel.com/Wemissyou.html.

Desborough, James, and Christopher Bucktin. "Michael Jackson Could Not Sing and Dance Live at the Same Time, Claim Emails to Be Presented in Court." *Mirror*, May 13, 2013. http://www.mirror.co.uk/news/world-news/michael-jackson-could-not-sing-1886104.

Deutsch, Linda. "Michael Jackson's Chef Recalls His Doctor's Role, His Diet, His Children and the Day He Died." HuffingtonPost.com, August 29, 2009. http://www.huffingtonpost.com/2009/07/29/michael-jacksons-chef-rec_n_246771.html.

Dobuzinskis, Alex. "Michael Jackson Concerts May Face Legal Challenge." Reuters.com, May 11, 2009. http://ca.reuters.com/article/idCATRE54A5CY20090511.

Duke, Alan. "Anesthesiologist: Michael Jackson Recruited Me to Help with Insomnia." CNN.com, August 22, 2013. http://www.cnn.com/2013/08/22/showbiz/michael-jackson-death-trial/.

———. "Autopsy Reveals Michael Jackson's Secrets." CNN.com, May 7, 2013. http://www.cnn.com/2013/05/07/showbiz/jackson-death-trial/.

———. "'I hurt,' Michael Jackson Says 6 Weeks Before Death." CNN.com, October 5, 2011. http://www.cnn.com/2011/10/05/justice/california-conrad-murray-trial/.

———. "Judge Rejects E-Mail Ban in Michael Jackson Death Lawsuit." CNN.com, November 8, 2012. http://www.cnn.com/2012/11/08/showbiz/jackson-aeg-ruling/.

———. "Michael Jackson Slurred His Speech After Visits to Dr. Klein, Aides Say." CNN.com, September 29, 2011. http://www.cnn.com/2011/09/28/justice/california-conrad-murray-trial/.

———. "Michael Jackson's Mom Remembers Her 'Sweet Little Boy.'" CNN.com, August 29, 2013. http://www.cnn.com/2013/08/29/showbiz/michael-jackson-birthday/.

———. "'Miracle' of Michael Jackson's Concert Announcement Described." CNN.com, June 13, 2013. http://www.cnn.com/2013/06/12/showbiz/jackson-death-trial/.

_____. " 'Perfect Storm' of Drugs Killed Michael Jackson, Sleep Expert Says." CNN.com, October 14, 2011. http://www.cnn.com/2011/10/13/justice/california-conrad-murray-trial/.

_____. "Promoter's E-Mail: Michael Jackson's Dermatologist 'Scares Us to Death.'" CNN.com, June 12, 2013. http://edition.cnn.com/2013/06/11/showbiz/jackson-death-trial/.

_____, with Mallory Simon. "Coroner's Preliminary Finding: Jackson Overdosed on Propofol." CNN.com, August 25, 2009. http://www.cnn.com/2009/SHOWBIZ/Music/08/24/michael.jackson.propofol/index.html?eref=onion.

Edwin, Bruce. "Interview with Michael Jackson Guitarist David Williams," 2009. *Hollywood Sentinel* (accessed March 24, 2015). http://www.thehollywoodsentinel.com/72809article5.html.

_____. "Michael Jackson Guitarist Called Conrad Murray Evil." News Blaze.com, October 2, 2011. http://newsblaze.com/story/2011100 2112510ente.nb/topstory.html.

"Fan Testimonies: What They Saw and Heard from Michael Himself." Tini for Justice (blogger), January 24, 2010. http://www.this-is-not-it.com/.

Ferry, Bryan. "David Williams — Bryan Ferry & Roxy Music 1986–2009." http://www.bryanferry.com/david-williams/.

"Former Longtime Jackson Insider Speaks Out." ABCNews.go.com, June 23, 2005. http://abcnews.go.com/GMA/MichaelJackson/story?id=874357.

Friedman, Roger. "Jacko Nanny Departs: Grace Is Gone." Showbiz411 .com, August 24, 2009. http://www.showbiz411.com/2009/08/24/20090824jacko-nanny-departs-grace-is-gone.

_____. "Jacko Plays the Apollo." FoxNews.com, April 25, 2002. http://www.foxnews.com/story/2002/04/25/jacko-plays-apollo.html.

_____. "Jacko Shows Delayed, but Are Definitely On." Showbiz411.com, May 11, 2009. http://www.showbiz411.com/2009/05/11/20090511jacko -michael-jackson-london-shows-delayed.

_____. "Michael Jackson Recorded a New Album in 2007." Show-biz411.com, May 2, 2010. http://www.showbiz411.com/2010/05/02/exclusive-michael-jackson-recorded-a-new-album-in-2007.

_____. "Michael Jackson's Nanny Locks His Father Out." FoxNews.com, January 31, 2007. http://www.foxnews.com/story/2007/01/31/michael-jackson-nanny-locks-his-father-out.

Galloway, Stephen. "Quincy Jones Recalls 'Freaking Out' at Michael Jackson's Death and His Private Nickname for the Star (Q&A)." HollywoodReporter.com, April 11, 2015. http://www.hollywoodreporter.com/news/quincy-jones-recalls-michael-jacksons-787976.

Gardner, David. "Conrad Murray's Mistress Describes Moment the Doctor Ended Their Phone Call When He Discovered Michael Jackson's Heart Had Stopped." DailyMail.com, October 4, 2011. http://www.dailymail.co.uk/news/article-2045280/Michael-Jackson-trial-Conrad-Murrays-mistress-describes-moment-doctor-discovered-popstars-heart-stopped.html.

Gardner, Eriq. "Michael Jackson's Former Publicist Can't Revive $44 Million Lawsuit." Billboard.com, May 13, 2014. https://www.billboard.com/biz/articles/news/legal-and-management/6084866/michael-jackson-publicist-raymone-brain-sultan-of-brunei-44-million.

Geller, Uri. "When Uri Met David." Telegraph.co.uk, December 31, 2001. http://www.telegraph.co.uk/culture/4728720/When-Uri-met-David.html.

Gorgan, Elena. "Michael Jackson Working with David Copperfield for Levitation Act." Softpedia.com, April 2, 2009. http://news.softpedia.com/news/Michael-Jackson-Working-with-David-Copperfield-for-Levitation-Act-108462.shtml.

Gould, Lara, and Will Payne. "World Exclusive: Jackson's Secret Girlfriend Was His Children's Former Nanny Grace Rwaramba." *Daily Mirror*, July 5, 2009. http://www.mirror.co.uk/3am/celebrity-news/world-exclusive-jacksons-secret-girlfriend-404397.

Grammy.com. http://www.grammy.com/artist/michael-jackson.

Heller, Corinne. "OTRC: Conrad Murray Trial: Michael Jackson's Slurred Voice Heard in Longer Recording, Singer Says: 'I Had No Childhood' (Audio)." ABC7.com. http://abc7.com/archive/8380098/.

"Historical Weather for 2009 in Los Angeles, California, USA." WeatherSpark.com. https://weatherspark.com/history/30699/2009/ Los-Angeles-California-United-States.

"Illusionist David Blaine on Sneaking into Parliament with Michael Jackson." HuffingtonPost.com, November 18, 2013. http://www .huffingtonpost.com/2013/11/18/david-blaine-michael-jackson _n_4297951.html.

Interview with Jermaine Jackson. IslamReligion.com, January 16, 2006. http://www.islamreligion.com/articles/90/jermaine-jackson-usa -part-1/.

"Jacko: I Won't Screw Over My Family." TMZ.com, June 2, 2009. http://www.tmz.com/2009/06/02/jacko-i-wont-screw-over-my -family/.

"Jackson Family Claims MJ Fired Branca." TMZ.com, October 1, 2009. http://www.tmz.com/2009/10/01/michael-jackson-john-branca -probate-howard-weitzman-katherine-jackson-brian-oxman/.

"Jackson Nanny Denies Pumping His Stomach." CBSNews.com, June 30, 2009. http://www.cbsnews.com/news/jackson-nanny-denies -pumping-his-stomach/.

"The Jacksons Deny Any Involvement with Planned Jackson 5 Reunion Show in Texas with Brother Michael and Sister Janet." MJackson .com, May 18, 2009. http://mjackson.com/the-jacksons-deny-any -involvement-with-planned-jackson-5-reunion-show-in-texas-with -brother-michael-a-sister-janet/.

Joseph, Jessi, Don Lemon, Jeff Reid, and Brian Larch. "Michael Jackson: The Final 24 Hours." CNN.com, June 23, 2010. http://www .cnn.com/2010/SHOWBIZ/Music/06/22/michael.jackson.final .hours/index.html.

Kaufman, Gil. "Michael Jackson's Final Hours: A Timeline." MTV .com, August 25, 2009. http://www.mtv.com/news/1619446/michael -jacksons-final-hours-a-timeline/.

McDonald, Sam. "Friends Remember Local Guitar Hero." DailyPress
.com, March 10, 2009. http://articles.dailypress.com/2009-03-10/
news/0903090089_1_cardiac-arrest-hampton-guitar.

"Michael Jackson: 100 Facts About the King of Pop." Telegraph.co.uk,
June 26, 2009. http://www.telegraph.co.uk/culture/music/michael
-jackson/5649814/Michael-Jackson-100-facts-about-the
-king-of-pop.html.

"Michael Jackson Drops Copperfield from His Show." AZCentral.com,
May 8, 2009. http://archive.azcentral.com/ent/celeb/articles/2009/
05/08/20090508jackson.html.

"Michael Jackson: His Final Days." Transcript of CNN Live Event/
Special. CNN.com, June 22, 2014. http://www.cnn.com/TRAN
SCRIPTS/1406/22/se.01.html.

"Michael Jackson Is 'Bad' with Animals." PETA, March 26, 2009.
http://www.peta.org/blog/michael-jackson-bad-animals/.

"Michael Jackson Leaves Animals Out of the Act." PETA, April 9, 2009.
http://www.peta.org/blog/michael-jackson-leaves-animals-act/.

"Michael Jackson Leaves London March 2009." MJJStreet.com, March
8, 2015. Blog. http://home.mjjstreet.com/blog/michael-jackson
-leaves-london-march-2009/.

"Michael Jackson Returns to Stage." BBC News, November 16, 2006.
http://news.bbc.co.uk/2/hi/entertainment/6152976.stm.

"Michael Jackson Sighting at Antique Store on April 22, 2009, in
Hollywood, California." Getty Images. Photograph. http://www
.gettyimages.com/detail/news-photo/michael-jackson-sighting-at
-antique-store-on-april-22-2009-news-photo/86364041.

"Michael Jackson Wants Apology After BBC Compared Him to IRA."
Telegraph.co.uk, March 20, 2009. http://www.telegraph.co.uk/cul
ture/music/michael-jackson/5020682/Michael-Jackson-wants
-apology-after-BBC-compared-him-to-IRA.html.

"Michael Jackson's Business Partner John Branca Looks to Rebuild
Singer's Finances, Legacy." Cleveland.com, August 25, 2012. http://
blog.cleveland.com/ent_impact_music/print.html?entry=/2012/
08/michael_jacksons_business_part.html.

"Michael Jackson's Final Hours." CBSNews.com, June 21, 2010. http://www.cbsnews.com/news/michael-jacksons-final-hours/.

"Michael Jackson's Latest Hit... and Run?" TMZ.com, April 23, 2009. http://www.tmz.com/2009/04/23/michael-jacksons-latest-hit-and-run/#ixzz3jgBdTQC6.

"Michael Jackson's Magician Identified." Magic Newswire, May 15, 2009. http://www.linkingpage.com/magicnewsfeed/2009/5/15/michael-jacksons-magician-identified.html.

"Michael Jackson's Word—Worthless?" TMZ.com, June 2, 2009. http://www.tmz.com/2009/06/02/michael-jacksons-word-worthless/#ixzz3bwKD7sMG.

Michaels, Sean. "Michael Jackson Planned Album of Classical Music." TheGuardian.com, July 3, 2009. http://www.theguardian.com/music/2009/jul/03/michael-jackson-classical-music-album.

"MJ Estate Coughed Up $55,000 to Pay Off 'Thriller' Chick." TMZ.com, January 4, 2013. http://www.tmz.com/2013/01/04/michael-jackson-estate-thriller-ola-ray-royalties-settlement/.

Murray, Conrad. Email to AEG Live tour accountant Timm Woolley, May 15, 2009.

muzikfactorytwo.blogspot.com.

"Prince Jefri Bolkiah's Las Vegas Mega-Compound." HomesOfThe Rich.net, August 11, 2008. http://homesoftherich.net/2008/08/prince-jefri-bolkiahs-las-vegas-mega-compound/.

"Raymone Bain Sues Michael Jackson for $44 Million." Washington Post.com, May 6, 2009. http://voices.washingtonpost.com/reliable-source/2009/05/rs-jackson7.html.

"Report: Michael Jackson Says He's Too Thin for 50-Concert Tour." FoxNews.com, June 2, 2009. http://www.foxnews.com/story/2009/06/02/report-michael-jackson-says-too-thin-for-50-concert-tour.html.

Roberts, Johnnie L. "Fired, the Superlawyer Returns to Bail Jackson Out—for a Price." TheWrap.com, December 8, 2010. http://www.thewrap.com/michael-jackson-4-brancas-fired-rehired-fired-22423/.

_____. "A Superlawyer Returns, a Pop Icon Dies—a Will Is Discovered." TheWrap.com, December 9, 2010. http://www.thewrap.com/michael-jackson-5-return-branca-22424/.

Siegel, Dick. "Inside the Tragic Death of Disney Child Star Bobby Driscoll." NationalEnquirer.com, December 4, 2014. http://www.nationalenquirer.com/celebrity/inside-tragic-death-disney-child-star-bobby-driscoll-peter-pan.

Simmons, Sylvie. "Michael Jackson: 'Magic Is Easy if You Put Your Heart into It'—a Classic Interview from the Vaults." TheGuardian.com, November 20, 2012. http://www.theguardian.com/music/2012/nov/20/michael-jackson-classic-interview.

"Singer Jackson Whipped by Father." BBC News, November 13, 2003. http://newsvote.bbc.co.uk/mpapps/pagetools/print/news.bbc.co.uk/2/hi/entertainment/3268133.stm.

Smith, Lizzie. "Wacko for Jacko: Michael Jackson Mobbed as He Takes His Children to See Oliver!" DailyMail.com, March 7, 2009. http://www.dailymail.co.uk/tvshowbiz/article-1160101/Wacko-Jacko-Michael-Jackson-mobbed-takes-children-Oliver.html.

Smith, Tim. "More Details on Instrumental Album Michael Jackson Started Before His Death." BaltimoreSun.com, July 10, 2009. http://weblogs.baltimoresun.com/entertainment/classicalmusic/2009/07/more_details_on_instrumental_a.html.

"'Thriller' Actress Ola Ray Paid $75,000 in Royalties Dispute: Report." Billboard.com, January 4, 2013. http://www.billboard.com/articles/news/1481596/thriller-actress-ola-ray-paid-75000-in-royalties-dispute-report.

TeamMichaelJackson.com.

Vindicating Michael. Blog. vindicatemj.wordpress.com/.

Vineyard, Jennifer. "Michael Jackson Shocks Al Sharpton by Calling Tommy Mottola a Racist." MTV.com, July 8, 2002. http://www.mtv.com/news/1455976/michael-jackson-shocks-al-sharpton-by-calling-tommy-mottola-a-racist/.

Vogel, Joseph. "The Return of the King." Slate.com, May 13, 2014. http://www.slate.com/articles/arts/culturebox/2014/05/rodney

_darkchild_jerkins_produces_michael_jackson_s_song_xscape
.html.

Whitcraft, Teri, Kristin Pisarcik, and Kimberly Brown. "TIMELINE: Michael Jackson's Final Days." ABCNews.com, June 23, 2010. http://abcnews.go.com/2020/MichaelJackson/michael-jackson -final-days-timeline-year-death-king/print?id=10974394.

Yoshino, Kimi, and Andrew Blankstein. "'Lethal Levels' of Anesthetic Propofol Killed Michael Jackson." LATimesBlogs, August 24, 2009. http://latimesblogs.latimes.com/lanow/2009/08/lethal-levels -of-anesthetic-propofol-killed-michael-jackson.html.

Video Sources

Bad 25. Dir. Spike Lee. ABC, 2012.

Conrad Murray's phone recording of Michael Jackson on May 10, 2009. YouTube (accessed June 2, 2015). https://www.youtube.com/ watch?v=x3nBDVxOW80.

"Jermaine Jackson Talks About His Islam on Al-Arabiya Channel with Suhair Al-Qaissy." YouTube (accessed March 31, 2015). https:// www.youtube.com/watch?v=4-cF9B-J8jU.

Live from Neverland Valley — 1993. YouTube (accessed March 27, 2015). https://www.youtube.com/watch?v=w270PK4o2_c.

Living with Michael Jackson: A Tonight Special. Dir. Julie Shaw. ABC, 2003.

"Michael Jackson and His Children: Prince, Paris and Blanket at Tom's Toys — May 15, 2009." YouTube (accessed May 30, 2015). https://www.youtube.com/watch?v=hDQ_R_yBMrs.

"Michael Jackson at the BET 2003 for James Brown HQ." YouTube (accessed March 19, 2015). https://www.youtube.com/watch?v =ZN48lsXL1oA.

"Michael Jackson — Dangerous Live at Apollo, 2002." C-SPAN (accessed March 19, 2015). http://www.dailymotion.com/ video/x9wowt_michael-jackson-dangerous-live-at-a_music.

"Michael Jackson — 'I Got the Feelin',' 1968." YouTube (accessed April 14, 2015). https://www.youtube.com/watch?v=Ux3joe0GdTA#t=47.

Michael Jackson: The Life of an Icon. Dir. Andrew Eastel. Universal Pictures. DVD, 2011.

"Michael Jackson—World Music Awards 2006." YouTube (accessed March 18, 2015). https://www.youtube.com/watch?v=WviiygVo3Oc.

Michael's First Christmas. FOX, 1993. YouTube (accessed April 7, 2015). https://www.youtube.com/watch?v=h0ewQrp2jWw.

MTV Most Wanted. Interview with David Williams. YouTube (accessed March 24, 2015). https://www.youtube.com/watch?v=JPodK48YRZA.

This Is It. Dir. Kenny Ortega. Sony Pictures Home Entertainment. DVD, 2009.

The Wiz. Dir. Sidney Lumet. Universal Studios Home Entertainment. DVD, 1999.

Personal Conversations

Areheart, Shaye

Charles, Ray

Dileo, Frank

Gaye, Marvin

Gordy, Berry

Jackson, Janet

Jackson, Katherine

James, Rick

Jones, Bob

Kawashima, Dale

Kelly, R.

Kravitz, Lenny

Phillinganes, Greg

Robinson, Smokey

Roshkind, Michael

Taylor, Bobby

Yetnikoff, Walter

Index

insomnia, 103, 108, 140, 147–48,
    163, 223–25
"In the Closet" (song; MJ), 105
Invincible (album; MJ), 26, 39, 60,
    79–80, 92
Ireland, 31, 33–34, 154
Irving, Washington, 136
isolation, 22, 83, 111–12,
    154, 156
"I Wanna Be Where You Are"
    (song; MJ), 26
"I Want You Back" (song;
    Jackson 5), 14, 17

Jackson, Blanket (son), 7, 65–66,
    107, 169
Jackson, Jackie (brother), 169, 173
Jackson, Janet (sister), 7, 24–25,
    29, 40, 110, 112, 115, 123,
    167–70
Jackson, Jermaine (brother), 30,
    53, 142, 169–70
Jackson, Jesse, 32
Jackson, Joseph (father), 28–29,
    31–33, 39–41, 46–52, 58–59,
    160, 167–68
  brutality of, 16, 46, 49–50, 61,
    75, 95, 134–35
  Michael and, 40, 61–62,
    75–82, 87–89, 156, 165,
    212–13, 234–35
  reunion concert and, 33,
    63–64, 76–78, 80, 82, 88–89,
    91, 123–24, 170–72

Jackson, Katherine (mother),
    46–52, 75–78, 82, 113–14,
    167–68, 229–31, 241
  manipulation by, 76, 89, 95,
    123–24, 170–72
  Michael and, 14, 41, 46–49,
    75, 78, 88–89, 178
Jackson, La Toya (sister), 30,
    169–70
Jackson, Marlon (brother),
    169, 173
Jackson, Michael (MJ)
  altruism of, 40, 56–57, 81, 164,
    178, 221–22
  ambition of, 4, 15–16, 62,
    68–69, 95–98, 105, 164–65,
    218, 234
  anxiety of, 140, 154–55, 163,
    180, 198, 203–4, 223–25
  appearance and, 36, 79–80,
    99–101, 155, 200, 202,
    221–22
  artistry of, 10, 26–27, 49, 127,
    232, 240
  childhood of, 14, 26, 29, 61,
    65, 111–13, 134–35, 165,
    178, 200, 231–32
  children of, 5, 13–14, 27–28,
    45, 53, 65–66, 113–15, 139,
    157, 180, 191–92, 230, 235
  collaboration with, 16, 96,
    104–5, 162, 234
  confidence of, 10, 155, 190,
    204, 210, 218, 231

About the Authors

TAVIS SMILEY is the host and managing editor of *Tavis Smiley* on PBS and *The Tavis Smiley Show* from Public Radio International (PRI). He is also the bestselling author of eighteen books. Smiley lives in Los Angeles.

DAVID RITZ, who collaborated on Smiley's *What I Know for Sure*, *Death of a King*, and *My Journey with Maya*, has worked with everyone from Ray Charles and Marvin Gaye to Aretha Franklin and B.B. King.